ETHICS A–Z

Forthcoming Volumes in the Philosophy A–Z Series

Chinese Philosophy A–Z, Bo Mou
Christian Philosophy A–Z, Daniel Hill
Epistemology A–Z, Martijn Blaauw and Duncan Pritchard
Feminist Philosophy A–Z, Nancy McHugh
Indian Philosophy A–Z, Christopher Bartley
Islamic Philosophy A–Z, Peter Groff
Jewish Philosophy A–Z, Aaron Hughes
Metaphysics A–Z, Peter Groff
Philosophical Logic A–Z, J. C. Beall
Philosophy of Language A–Z, Allessandro Tanesini
Philosophy of Law & Legal Theory A–Z, Patrick O'Donnell
Philosophy of Mind A–Z, Marina Rakova
Philosophy of Religion A–Z, Patrick Quinn
Philosophy of Science A–Z, Stathis Psillos

Ethics A–Z

Jonathan A. Jacobs

Edinburgh University Press

© Jonathan A. Jacobs, 2005

Edinburgh University Press Ltd
22 George Square, Edinburgh

Typeset in 10.5/13 Sabon
by TechBooks India, and printed and
bound in Finland by WS Bookwell

A CIP record for this book is
available from the British Library

ISBN 0 7486 2196 2 (hardback)
ISBN 0 7486 2014 1 (paperback)

Contents

Series Editor's Preface

One of the aspects of ethics that makes it so interesting is its combination of high theory and the very practical experiences we have when doing things. Our actions can be analysed using a wide variety of ethical criteria, many of which we do not think about when acting, and yet at the same time those actions themselves are very familiar to us. The more we know about our actions, the more we know about ourselves, or so it is often thought. Yet ethics introduces ways of seeing our actions that may bring out features which we never really considered as important or even relevant. The subtle distinctions that ethics can make are very revealing when we examine our actions and try to place them within a broader theoretical framework. It is this subtlety that makes a book like this so useful, since we find here a careful delineation of many important thinkers and ideas. The Chinese philosopher Mencius might be right when he said that moral principles please our minds as beef and mutton and pork please our mouths, but it is a lot easier to identify tasty food than it is to understand what is the right action in a particular situation. Jonathan Jacobs's book is designed to lay out the variety of theories and personalities in the field of ethics. Not every significant thinker or theory will be discussed, but some of the most important are contained here. This book will be a useful accompaniment to the study of ethics, and brings out nicely the varying perspectives which exist within the discipline.

Oliver Leaman

Introduction

Ethics A–Z is meant to be a resource for students and other readers at various levels of the study of ethical theory. It does not claim to be exhaustive, but I hope to have included entries that really are essential and also many that may be helpful to those whose study ranges a bit more widely. It is certainly not a substitute for the reading of primary texts but it will, I hope, prove to be a congenial companion to those texts and the readers of them. For those who are just coming to the subject (philosophy in general or ethics in particular), the book should help you negotiate concepts, positions, and arguments that may be new to you. For those already under way in thinking philosophically about ethics, the book should prove to contain informative and clarifying reminders, cross-references, and synopses. Most entries are quite brief, but the cross-referencing should enable you to pursue matters in somewhat more depth.

The order of entries is strictly alphabetical; the book is not organised topically or chronologically. Also, a quick examination will reveal that there are entries for thinkers, for positions, for key arguments, and for some specific moral issues. There are relatively few of the last. This is a guide to the philosophical study of ethics, and so it mostly concerns how moral issues are thought about, rather than being directly concerned with moral problems as such. A small number of moral problems have been included because they are especially apt and effective in raising or illustrating important philosophical positions or arguments. So, for example, there are entries for 'punishment' and 'euthanasia' but not for 'honesty' or 'generosity'. The latter two are certainly of considerable moral importance. Still, the former two merit inclusion because of how they can be used to exhibit fundamental theoretical distinctions. They are also more controversial than honesty and generosity, and the controversies have to do with the quite fundamental issues they raise.

The overall philosophical study of ethics can be broken down into normative ethics, metaethics, and moral psychology. These are not sealed compartments separated by clean breaks, but they are helpful categories for bringing different aspects of ethics into view. While a number of issues straddle these categories, they can help us to see more clearly what sorts of questions those issues address or raise. Normative ethics concerns what is right and wrong, obligatory or prohibited, just or unjust. That is, normative ethics concerns substantive ethical matters. The claim that capital punishment is justified in at least some cases (whatever one's view of the correctness of the claim) is a normative claim. To assert that it is always wrong to make a deceitful promise is to make a normative claim. If you maintain that we ought to show gratitude to benefactors, you are holding a position on a normative matter.

On the other hand, the claim that moral rightness and wrongness are objective features of actions (in contrast to being grounded in feelings or attitudes or being matters of cultural convention) is not a substantive moral claim. It is a claim about the status of moral features, and as such, it is a metaethical claim. Metaethics is concerned with the interpretation of moral discourse, questions concerning the status of moral values (as objective or subjective, and in what senses), and crucial features of moral judgements, including the issue of whether they are cognitive judgements or not. Overall, metaethics is concerned with the metaphysics, semantics and epistemology of morality. Its issues include the question of whether moral judgements are literally true or false by virtue of moral facts, or are to be evaluated on some other basis. Would that other basis be norms that are culture-bound but not universally or objectively justifiable? If there are moral facts and properties, how are they related to non-moral facts and properties? If values are subjective, how are we to explain the weight and authority of moral considerations? Is there such a thing as an increase or improvement in moral knowledge, or are there just changes in the values people accept?

You will find numerous entries in *Ethics A–Z* that concern metaethical positions, distinctions and concepts. Indeed, during the last century much of the most important work and many of the most prominent philosophical arguments in ethics have been in metaethics or have at least included substantial metaethical elements. For instance, there is considerable debate over the issue of where moral value is 'located'. Is it in the states of affairs actions bring about, or is it an intrinsic feature of an action, or is value present in some other manner? A theory that holds that moral value is to be found in the states of affairs produced by actions (rather than, say, the agent's motives) is a *consequentialist* theory. Accordingly, there are entries on consequentialism and numerous other positions on the question of the locus of moral value. While there has been a striking increase in attention to normative issues in recent decades on the part of philosophers, there are some key metaethical issues that remain central to the philosophical agenda.

In addition, numerous topics in ethics come under the heading 'moral psychology'. These include such matters as the nature and moral significance of happiness, pleasure, self-respect and weakness of will. Explorations of regret, self-mastery, shame, self-love and friendship are projects in moral psychology. Also, the debate about the unity of the virtues, i.e. whether an agent can fully have one or another virtue (courage, perhaps) without also having others (such as practical wisdom and justice) is in the sphere of moral psychology. The positions and arguments having to do with self-interest and altruism are matters of moral psychology. Is it necessary to show that being moral is in one's self-interest in order for that person to be rationally committed to morality? While this is not the book to answer that question it includes material on the issues involved in it. Accounts of the role of sensibility and affect in moral judgement and moral motivation are within the ambit of moral psychology as well as that of metaethics.

The nature of moral motivation is one of the fundamental issues of moral psychology. Some theorists maintain that reason or understanding alone cannot move us to act rightly. In their view being moved to act requires some desire, feeling or attitude that is not entirely a matter of belief, not entirely a cognitive matter. Others hold that insofar as we are rational, we will act on what we understand to be moral considerations. In that view, a failure to be moral is a failure of rationality rather than a matter of not having the right sort of desire or sensibility. This question of how moral beliefs and commitments are related to action is of the first importance in theorising about ethics because ethics concerns what we are to *do*. Whether moral motivation is grounded in sensibility, reason, choice or desire we need an account of what it takes to move us effectively to act in ways responsive to moral considerations. The position called 'internalism' holds that the acknowledgement of the reasons why an action is morally required also has (at least some) motivational efficacy. 'Externalists' argue that the content of moral considerations on the one hand and motivational efficacy on the other, are independent of each other. One could fully understand the moral reasons in favour of acting in a certain way in a situation, without being moved to act that way just on account of that understanding. The book includes material on that debate and its relations to other issues.

There are several entries in *Ethics A–Z* that concern the sorts of features that may not be emphasised in a first course in ethics, but are nonetheless of the first importance. Beyond the introductory level such features appropriately receive increasing attention because of how significant they are for understanding moral theorising.

There are also some entries for topics that may not be easy to categorise, but are certainly important to ethical thought. The issue of fortune is an instance of this. Fortune concerns the ways in which, and the extent to which, we do not have complete control over our actions, and perhaps for that reason, do not have complete control over the moral worth or moral significance of our actions. It also concerns those features of our character and our circumstances over which we do not have control. For example, some of us have our courage severely tested, while others do not. Even if the term 'fortune' (or its counterpart in another language) is not used, the topic is of long-standing and is treated in some of the most influential moral thought. That is certainly the case for Aristotle and Kant, just to mention two key thinkers. Another topic meriting attention is amoralism. Exploration of amoralism can help bring into view what sorts of concern or understanding must be present in a moral agent. Conceptualising and describing an amoral agent – one with no moral commitments or no genuine concern for morality – can bring into view more clearly what an agent must be like in order to be a participant in the moral order. The amoralist is different from the morally bad or corrupt person, and different from the weak-willed agent as well. Considering why, and discriminating between these categories has considerable value for the ways in which it helps us ascertain what is required for moral agency and for well-formed moral agency.

As your study of ethics progresses you are likely to find yourself recognising issues and arguments as mainly belonging to normative theory or to metaethics or to moral psychology. You are also likely to notice connections between various issues and positions, and the several pathways of implication, mutual support (or exclusion) and presupposition. If *Ethics A–Z* 'works' properly, it will support you at any and all stages of that progress and it will assist you in bringing a complex but also increasingly interconnected conceptual map into view.

I should note that this is a book on Western thinkers and their formulations of the issues. That is the living tradition (it is really many traditions) I know best, and it is almost certainly the body of material on which your own study is focused. It is likely that many of the entries are already somewhat familiar to you (e.g. Aristotle or utilitarianism) while there are others you may have heard of (such as the state of nature or the Cambridge Platonists) but do not know well. The length of an entry is not a straightforward indicator of its importance. If the main points about a topic or figure can be stated very briefly, the entry will be brief, even if it concerns a quite important topic or person. The entries are intended to be mutually reinforcing, and there is a good deal of cross-referencing in the book. That makes it possible to pursue matters to different levels of detail and scope, and to make connections between different dimensions of theorising about morality – its metaethics and its moral psychology, for example.

Also, while I have tried to supply explications that are clear and accurate, it is important to remember that many of the entries are themselves matters of philosophical dispute. For example, there are competing conceptions of realism; there are disputes about the nature of justice, and about how to interpret the role of conscience. Moreover, even if a certain approach or theoretical position, such as consequentialism, or retributivism, can be articulated clearly, that does not imply that it usually occurs in a 'pure' form. It could be that many important consequentialists also acknowledge some other kinds of considerations in ascertaining moral requirements. It may

be that in many of the theories in which retributivism is prominent, other considerations also have a role. This is not because
those theorists have betrayed their own principles or are guilty
of inconsistencies. That *may* be; but it must be ascertained on
the basis of careful scrutiny. If theories were always 'pure'
they would be much less interesting than they are and almost
certainly less responsive to the complexity of the phenomena
they attempt to render intelligible. My hope is that *Ethics A–Z*
will help you to comprehend better the phenomena and the
theories that address them. It is not an attempt at supplying
you with a neat and unproblematic set of facts and definitions
that somehow do the work for you.

Finally, some remarks about the form of the entries. Within
each entry, terms in bold print indicate that those topics are
also individually in the book. The same is done with the names
of thinkers. If you see '**Kant**' in the entry on '**universalisation**',
you will find a separate entry for '**Kant**'. In addition, at the
end of most entries, other relevant entries are indicated by
'See'. If a term is in bold print in the body of an entry it is
not also listed in 'See'. There are some cases in which the term
in bold print in the body of an entry is not exactly the same
as the term for the corresponding entry. For example, if you
find '**consequentialist**' in the body of an entry, its appropriate
cross-reference is '**consequentialism**'. If '**Platonic**' occurs in an
entry, its cross-reference is '**Plato**'. I have done that where the
cross-reference is important but the grammar of the sentence
required that the term have a specific ending.

The last part of each entry is 'Further reading'. For any
thinker who is listed there or whose name is in bold print in
the entry, there is information on relevant readings in the Bibliography. Some of the 'Further reading' entries include only
primary sources authored by the person discussed, while some
others identify important secondary sources. In fact, there are
a small number of people who are included in 'Further reading' who do not have their own entries in the main body of the

book. That is because there is some book or article of theirs that is particularly important to a certain topic. This is especially true of some contemporary thinkers. There is a great deal of work being done in ethics in our time. *Ethics A–Z* acknowledges that while taking a broad view of the history of philosophy; it is not meant to be mainly a survey of recent and contemporary literature. Also, the Bibliography is a bibliography for this book, not for ethics overall. It will guide you to a good deal of the most important thinking, and many of the items cited have their own helpful bibliographies.

Readers may take exception to my decisions about what to include and how the entries have been treated. It would be amazing were that not the case. I have tried to be accurate and fair and I have tried to guard against 'taking sides' in any of the main debates in moral philosophy. *Ethics A–Z* is meant to aid you on your way deeper into those debates, rather than to provide any short cuts through them or easy ways around them.

Jonathan A. Jacobs

Acknowledgements

First of all I would like to express my thanks to Oliver Leaman, editor of the A–Z Series. His invitation to me to write this book was unexpected, but very welcome. Working on the project has been very gratifying in part for my having been asked to do the job by someone whose uncommonly broad and deep learning I respect a great deal. David McCabe, Jason Kawall, and Maude Clark – colleagues of mine in philosophy at Colgate University – read draft material and made numerous critical and helpful suggestions. Jean Getchonis assisted in preparing the manuscript. As always, the efficiency and quality of her work were not only very helpful but also rather like a friendly admonition.

Ethics A–Z

A

Abelard, Peter (1079–1142) French: Abelard gave an account of the moral value of actions as a matter of consent to what is right or wrong. The distinction between sinning – which is actually consenting to what is wrong – and the desire to do something that is wrong is crucial to Abelard. The consent is the proper target of moral condemnation. An action itself is morally indifferent in the sense that the moral wrongfulness does not lie in the commission of the act but in one's consent to do it. An act of killing or of taking someone's property without authorisation to do so could be done without sin. It could be done by mistake or forced upon one. When it is not done by mistake, it is the intention, the consent to the desire to do the thing that makes it morally wrong. The individual with natural predispositions and susceptibilities that make temperance extremely difficult may find himself yielding to desires he wishes he did not have. In one respect, he is doing what he wants to do, but in another respect he is caused (by his own dispositions and passions) to act in a way contrary to how he wishes to be moved. This agent sins, but involuntarily. As a rule, our actions are morally blameworthy or praiseworthy because we have the power to consent (or not) to the action guiding considerations accessible to us through belief, desire, and emotion. Abelard's approach to ethics was considered suspect in his time and he was condemned for heresy. However, elements of this sort of view were developed and articulated later, most notably by **Kant**.

See **consequentialism, non-consequentialism**
Further reading: Abelard 1971

absolutism: This is the view, with regard to a moral principle or claim, that it holds everywhere and is never overridden. For example, one might hold that the claim, 'harming another person just for the pleasure of doing so' is absolutely wrong. There are no exceptional cases, and in no case is the principle overridden. Moral absolutism is not the same as moral **objectivity**. Objectivity concerns the status of the considerations justifying the claim, and a moral claim can be objective but possibly overridden. For example, some theorists have argued that while it is objectively wrong deliberately to deceive another person, it may justifiable in certain circumstances. The wrongness of lying is not relative or subjective. Still, its wrongness is not automatically the most decisive moral consideration in a situation where there are other moral considerations as well. How a consideration figures in a given case may depend upon many features of the situation. In this approach, the view would be that the wrongness of deceit is an objective matter but not absolute. Contrariwise, **relativism** and **subjectivism** maintain that there are no objective moral considerations. The absolutist claims that there are some moral principles that hold *no matter what* the circumstances, and a condition that strong is not required by moral objectivism. It would be a little bit misleading to say that any moral theory in which there is a fundamental moral principle or criterion of right action is absolutist just by virtue of including such a principle. For example, according to the **utilitarian**, the principle of utility is held to apply everywhere at all times, but that is not quite the same as the principle being absolute. Absolutism is more helpfully understood as being a feature of specific moral rules, such as 'deceitful promise-making is wrong', or 'harming others just for the pleasure of it is wrong'. A moral theory may hold that there are no absolute principles even if it holds that there is a fundamental criterion of moral rightness and wrongness. It also seems that most of the principles that are regarded as absolute are prohibitions rather than injunctions to act in certain ways.

See **Kant,** *prima facie*
Further reading: Kant 1976; Kant 1980

act-utilitarianism: This is a version of utilitarianism according to which the decisive moral considerations are those that indicate what individual act in the specific circumstances is likely to produce the greatest **happiness** or utility. Individual acts, rather than general rules and principles, are the proper objects of moral concern and justification. The view is contrasted with rule-utilitarianism, an approach to moral deliberation that puts weight on following rules that are believed generally to promote utility. Defenders of act-utilitarianism argue that basing moral decision on other grounds – for example, the overall utility of people acting on the basis of general rules – is at odds with the basic commitments of **utilitarianism.** This is because doing so would permit actions that are known not to maximise utility. In *Utilitarianism* **Mill** does not distinguish between act and **rule-utilitarianism,** and there are passages and arguments that can be regarded as evidence of his holding each of the two views. The distinction was not explicitly made until some time after Mill wrote the work.

See **consequentialism**
Further reading: Mill 1979; Smart and Williams 1973

agent-centred considerations: Some moral theories hold that the scope of **impartiality** is appropriately restricted by considerations about individual agents' projects and concerns. Defenders of the view often criticise **utilitarian** theories (among others) for failing to acknowledge properly constraints on action grounded in agents' self-conceptions and limits on what they take to be morally allowable, at least for themselves. For example, a defender of agent-centred considerations might argue that (a) there are ways in which (utilitarian) good could be maximised, but that certain actions that would maximise it are morally out of the question, and that (b) there is a moral right that protects agents from criticism for not having taken the maximising action. Similar objections are often raised against some **Kantian**-inspired theories. In those theories strict regard to universalisable principles, without regard for particular agents and their central concerns and desires is taken to be the distinctively moral position. Here again, questions have been raised about whether impartiality should have an absolute claim over the way agents consider and respond to the moral considerations in a situation. The point is not that fairness is not morally required but that it is morally permissible to make one's utmost effort to attend to the needs of family or loved ones, even if doing so involves attending less to strangers one is in a position to aid more quickly and with better prospects of success. That kind of partiality is not a moral fault. In some views it is always permissible to act with a view to maximising the good, but it is also permissible to take a course that does not maximise good if doing so would conflict with an agent-centred consideration. That is not to say that we ought to maximise the good only if we feel like it, but that agents can have morally weighty reasons that justify a course of action that does not maximise good. If maximising required the agent knowingly to harm (or abandon to harm) some agents as part of the only course of action that would maximise good in the circumstances, the agent may be justified in insisting that morally, *he* cannot do that, even if others could.

See **agent-neutral considerations, Bentham, impartiality, Mill**

Further reading: Nozick 1974; Scheffler 1982

agent-neutral considerations: These are moral considerations that have weight without regard to the ends, concerns and commitments of particular individuals and their own judgement of the significance of those ends, concerns and commitments. For example, if a defender of **utilitarianism** argues that the single, decisive moral consideration is the extent to which an action contributes to the overall, aggregate utility, that position indicates that the utilitarian regards utility as agent-neutral. Agent-neutral considerations can be expressed in terms that are **universal** and **impartial**. The defender of agent-neutrality argues that if there are decisive agent-neutral considerations for doing X then I ought do X, even if doing so is contrary to my own central concerns and desires. The fact that my autonomy or the projects and aspirations important to me are at odds with strict impartiality does not get in the way of agent-neutral reasons for action. The dispute about whether all, or only parts, of morality are properly agent-neutral, is prominent in contemporary theorising. Defenders of **agent-centred considerations** will argue that not all of morality should be agent-neutral.

Further reading: Nagel 1986; Scheffler 1982; Williams 1981

altruism: Altruistic actions are those an agent performs for the good of others, for their sake, rather than for the good for herself. Altruism is often understood in contrast to **egoism**. As a moral obligation altruism requires us to promote the interests and well being of others even if we do not feel inclined to do so. In that respect it is not a feeling but a type of regard or concern. Altruistic actions can of course, be gratifying; we can enjoy doing good for others. But altruistic acts are not primarily means of promoting one's own interests or welfare or gratification. In many moral theories the possibility of altruism as a sustained, effective concern for others is a key issue, given what seem to be the very strong propensities of people to act self-interestedly. In the history of moral philosophy there are persistent debates over the question of whether altruism is rationally required or grounded in sensibility, in affect. Several thinkers in the early modern and modern tradition of British moralists argued that human beings have a natural tendency to care about the well being of others and that we do not need to argued out of egoism because we are not naturally egoistic. Other thinkers, such as **Kant,** sought to ground altruism in reason rather than sensibility and argued that promoting the ends of others and respecting them as autonomous agents is required by the very nature of practical reason. In addition, there are also important moral theories in which it is not directly raised at all. This is true of a great deal of ancient moral theory. This is not to say that those theories ignored duties to others or the importance of concern for well being that is not one's own. However, moral theorising influenced by religious traditions has tended to make it an issue that is crucial and explicit even when that theorising does not involve theological elements. The question of altruism's form and grounding concerns both moral value and moral motivation.

See **Hobbes, Hume, Hutcheson, Mill**

Further reading: Butler 1991; Hume 1975 and 1978; Nagel 1970

amoralism: The amoralist regards moral considerations as either wrongheaded, unimportant, or otherwise seriously objectionable. The amoralist is of interest because reflection on such an agent can be part of an exploration of how moral considerations can (or cannot) be motivating, and what kind of authority moral considerations do (or should) have for a rational agent. For instance, is the amoralist guilty of irrationality? If an amoral agent sees that certain considerations are regarded by others as morally decisive reasons, but this agent is unmoved by them, is that a failure of understanding, or does the amoralist simply lack certain feelings or concerns that others have and regard as important? In some respects the amoralist plays a role in ethics that is a counterpart to the role played by the sceptic in epistemology. In each case, consideration of that role is a method of testing the justifications of claims and seeing if they can meet certain important challenges. It can also be a way of testing whether those challenges are as genuine or as powerful as they are typically claimed to be. Consideration of the amoralist is an instructive way to explore what sorts of concerns and motives are needed in order for an agent to be a full-fledged (if not necessarily virtuous) participant in the moral world. **Kant** held that participation is a matter of rationality while others, such as **Hume,** held that it is a matter of having a certain kind of sensibility that is natural to us even if it needs to be extended and encouraged in certain ways. An exploration of amoralism can be illuminating in respect of whether the position is a rational option, something a rational agent might genuinely consider for adoption. A **weak-willed** agent recognises the weight of moral reasons but fails to act accordingly. The amoralist is simply unmoved by moral reasons – he does not see that they count in favour of the actions they point to as morally required. The amoralist is to be distinguished from the **vicious** agent. That is someone who is committed to moral values but they are wrong or perverse values.

Further reading: Brink 1989; Williams 1972

Anscombe, G. E. M. (1919–2001) English: Anscombe's works range across many areas of philosophy and she has had particular influence with regard to the explanation of human action and in Wittgenstein-influenced analytical philosophy in general. Her article, 'Modern Moral Philosophy', first published in 1958, is increasingly recognised as a turning-point of sorts in moral philosophy. In it she argued that the prevailing approaches to moral philosophy (**consequentialism** and **deontology**) are seriously inadequate and that a tenable moral theory must be firmly grounded in an adequate moral psychology – something she said philosophers had largely neglected. Also, her arguments in favour of **virtue-centred ethical theorising** (along with those of **Philippa Foot**) helped give impetus to that approach, and much of her own work involved deploying resources from **Aristotle** and **Aquinas**, as well as Wittgenstein, in contemporary debates. In Anscombe's own view the Aristotelian and Thomistic elements are joined to an explicit commitment to Catholicism, though in much of her writing she discusses key issues without introducing theological considerations.

Further reading: Anscombe 1958

anti-realism: This is interpreted in a number of ways and anti-realism in general can often best be described in terms of what it denies. In the context of ethics, anti-realism is the view that (a) moral values (or obligations or properties) do not exist in the way realists claim they do, that is, as independent of human affect, choice, responses or (b) that moral judgements (or claims or statements) are not to be interpreted as literally true or false (i.e. true or false in a fully objective sense) with regard to moral facts or values. The anti-realist might argue that to the extent that moral judgements are correct or justified that is a matter of how they stand with regard to people's norms and commitments rather than their being literally or objectively true or false. A common move in defence of anti-realism is to argue that **realism** is untenable in that it cannot satisfactorily account for the practical, action-guiding significance of moral considerations. To do that, those considerations must have a ground in something about us – desires, passions, or commitments; in something that has motivational efficacy. Beliefs and cognitions on their own do not have that efficacy, according to the anti-realist critique. Some anti-realists argue that moral values are relative rather than universal, and that no moral claims are *the* correct, or true ones, since there is no universal, objective measure of their rightness. Other anti-realists argue that all of the form and force of reason-giving, argument and rational revision of our moral views can be preserved and explained on anti-realist bases. They hold that realism about moral values is both untenable *and* unnecessary for the genuineness and significance of morality. An anti-realist could hold that moral statements are true or false relative to the norms that people endorse and accept, but the realist would regard that as a kind of relativism or subjectivism that does not involve truth and falsity in their proper senses. That would not be literal or objective truth and falsity. Thus, there is a wide range of views that fall under the 'anti-realist' heading, and they extend from views intended to explain away moral considerations to views meant to explain the authority of moral considerations without recourse to allegedly problematic objective values. **Expressivist** accounts of morality are anti-realist.

See **emotivism, Hume, projectivism, relativism, scepticism**

Further reading: Ayer 1952; Blackburn 1993 and 1998;

Hare 1963 and 1973; Hume 1975 and 1978; McDowell
1979, 1988 and 1997

a posteriori: A proposition or principle is *a posteriori* if it
is based upon empirical considerations or known to be
true (or false) on the basis of empirical evidence. This is
in contrast to claims held to be true (or false) independent of such evidence and solely on the basis of logical
form or conceptual analysis. Those claims and the methods of ascertaining their truth or falsity are *a priori*. Some
moral theories rely heavily on *a posteriori* considerations
about desires, sensibility, the nature of motivation and human beings' primary ends, concerns and interests. Hume's
moral theorising is an example of the extensive (but not
exclusive) reliance on *a posteriori* claims and method.
Much of the British moral tradition in general has a de-
cidedly *a posteriori* character. It is much less prominent
in the German tradition, for example. A great deal of
twentieth-century **metaethical** theorising relied centrally
on *a priori* claims and in particular, claims about the
meaning of moral discourse.

a priori: This can refer either to propositions and principles,
or to a way in which certain propositions and principles
are known. An *a priori* proposition is such that it can
be known to be true (or false) independent of empirical
evidence or testing. Many philosophers argue that math-
ematical propositions, for example, are *a priori*. (They
have in mind pure mathematics, not propositions of applied mathematics.) In contrast, propositions in chem-
istry, geography or cosmetology are *a posteriori*; they are
known on the basis of empirical inquiry and evidence. In
moral theory *a priori* propositions and principles may –
or may not – play a significant role in theorising. In
Kant's theory they are of the first importance. He held

that from an *a priori* analysis of the concept of rational agency and the concept of duty, the first principle of morality, the **categorical imperative**, could be ascertained. He also thought that a distinctive kind of respect owed to rational agents could be explicated just through examination of the concept of rational agency. Contrariwise, **utilitarianism** employs empirical methods in formulating and applying its fundamental claims. In the context of moral theorising a particularly important focus of *a priori* argument concerns questions about what it is rational to want or do, and the rational structure of ends, and whether there are any moral requirements that can be ascertained in those explorations. **Natural law** theorising often involves important *a priori* claims about rational agency. Also, questions about what is required by **impartiality** are often answered in ways that involve *a priori* reasoning. For example, this might involve revealing an inconsistency in a certain application of a purportedly impartial set of principles. There is often a complex mix of *a priori* and *a posteriori* considerations, as in **Aristotle**'s theorising. Of course, argumentation from given premises in any subject area often involves *a priori* reasoning. With regard to moral theory the main issue is whether the premises are, or are arrived at *a priori*. In addition, much of the debate about the meaning of moral discourse during the last 100 years involved *a priori* theorising about whether moral claims have truth values, and whether moral discourse refers to facts or expresses attitudes or stances.

See **Ayer, Hume, metaethics, Mill, Moore**

Further reading: Ayer 1952; Hume 1975 and 1978; Kant 1976; Mill 1979; Moore 1994

Aquinas, Thomas (1225–74) Italian: An enduringly influential Catholic theologian and philosopher, he understood philosophy to be in the service of theology. Nonetheless, many of his works have a considerable merit just in terms of their philosophical depth, rigour and insight. In his major works, *Summa Theologica* and *Summa Contra Gentiles*, there are substantial portions on moral psychology, the **virtues**, freedom of the **will** and human actions, the relation of the moral virtues to the intellectual and theological virtues, **natural law**, and human **happiness** and the proper end for human nature. He was strongly influenced by, and was an important commentator on **Aristotle** (in ethics as well as other areas).

Like Aristotle, he has an intellectualist conception of man's end; however, his conception of the being with whom we can be united is the God of Christianity, and the union with God requires the theological virtues. There is not any close counterpart to Christian grace in Aristotle's ethics or metaphysics, and there are no theological virtues (which, in Aquinas's view, have to be infused by God) in his moral psychology and conception of the soul. That said, there are very substantial affinities between Aristotle and Aquinas, and Aquinas certainly regarded Aristotle's thought as a pinnacle of rational understanding, though incomplete on account of not knowing of the Christian revelation. Because of the depth of his understanding of Aristotle and because of the richness of his own thought, Aquinas's works are attracting growing contemporary interest. It is increasingly recognised that it is not correct to regard Aquinas simply as 'Aristotle plus Christianity'. The interest in his ethical thought tends to be focused on its value to current developments and defences of **virtue-centred** moral psychology and moral theory.

See **Anscombe, Foot, MacIntyre, perfectionism**
Further reading: Aquinas 1966, 1983 and 1998

Aristotle (384–22 BCE) Greek: Aristotle's ethical theorising was influential in the Hellenistic period, in the later middle ages, and is very prominent in the contemporary setting. He developed a virtue-centred **eudaimonism**, a theory in which human flourishing and the virtuous activities required for it are the central concerns. His *Nicomachean Ethics* (and to a lesser extent, *Eudemian Ethics*) is a foundational work in **virtue-centred theorising**.

He argued that there is an intrinsic end proper to human nature, namely, *eudaimonia* (often translated as 'happiness') and that it is fundamentally grounded in rational activity. That includes both deliberative, practical activity and theoretical activity, intellectual activity for its own sake. Indeed, one of the main interpretive debates about Aristotle concerns the relation between the intellectualist ideal and the life of practical activity (in particular, ethical activity in civic life). Aristotle held that there are intellectual **virtues** and virtues of character, the latter acquired through habituation. There is, though, an important connection between the two kinds of virtues; practical wisdom (or **prudence**) is an action-guiding intellectual virtue. It is the understanding of human good that one needs in order to deliberate, choose and act well. Moreover, Aristotle held that one cannot fully have the virtues of character without practical wisdom, and vice versa.

Another key part of his view is that ethics cannot be codified, nor is there some single fundamental principle or criterion of right action, as there is in **Kant**'s or **Mill**'s theories, for example. The *phronimos*, the man of **practical wisdom**, is a living norm, and a proper object of emulation (which is not mere imitation). There are certain virtues the excellent person must have, and there are certain ethical rules the agent acts on, but ethics overall is a matter of judgement that is carefully calibrated to the features of particular situations. It is not simply or mainly a matter of rule-following.

Through Aristotle's influence, virtue-centred theorising often takes a form in which it is (a) **cognitivist,** (b) **particularist,** and (c) focused on what makes for a well-led life rather than fixed rules or principles of action. The notion of a flourishing, worthwhile life, shaped by sound habituation and well-ordered self-determination is central in Aristotle's theorising and most of the theorising influenced by it. Aristotle's ethics can be interpreted as a kind of **naturalism** because of the significance in it of a proper end, intrinsic to human nature. However, his conception of fully actualised intellectual activity is a conception of activity that transcends our biological human nature. Even leaving that aside, Aristotle's naturalism is quite different from other versions such as Mill's, for instance. According to the former, what we find most pleasing is found to be so because it is good – it is naturally pleasing as the proper activity of a being with our nature. According to the latter, pleasure is a psychological state, a type of experience, which is desirable for its own sake, and which is good as so desired. Moreover, **utilitarians** and many other theorists hold that there is a single, comprehensive criterion of right and wrong, while in Aristotle's ethical theorising the person with practical wisdom is the relevant measure. That person can articulate the reasons for his actions. In that sense there is moral understanding that can be transmitted. But those reasons are not themselves derivable from the application of an overall criterion of rightness.

See **Foot, MacIntyre, McDowell**

Further reading: Aristotle 1985; Foot 1978 and 2001; MacIntyre 1981; McDowell 1978 and 1979 *ataraxia*: In **Stoic** philosophy this is the state of tranquillity or imperturbability that is attained by achieving self-mastery. To a large extent, self-mastery is a matter of knowing how to value things so that one is not perturbed and agitated by things that do not merit concern. The recognition that **happiness** does not depend upon external goods, or indeed, that which we cannot control, is central. Epicurean philosophy also valued *ataraxia*, even though it endorsed a **hedonist** theory of value. **Epicurus** argued that happiness is not a matter of pleasing episodes, but rather sustained tranquillity. That condition is attainable through having a careful, reflective appreciation of what will contribute to pleasure of the best kind, in contrast to chasing after momentary, even if intense pleasures.

See **Stoicism**

Further reading: Aurelius 1989; Epictetus 1948; Epicurus 1994

Augustine (354–430 CE) North African: Strongly influenced by neo-Platonists, Augustine's thought has shaped some of the main currents of Christian thought since his time. In his rejection of the Manichean beliefs of his youth he developed a moral psychology and a metaphysics of morals centred around the belief that man's chief good is a loving union with God, the highest possible object of desire and striving. In this loving union with God the soul is virtuously ordered and loves only that which is fully satisfying and enduring. This notion of human nature as desiring and striving, and seeking peace in the fulfilment of desire was central to Augustine's conception of true peace and genuine perfection as possible only through love of God. Augustine also argued that each of us is capable of knowing the moral law, and that evil is brought into the world through disordered or perverse volition. Well-ordered volition is properly ordered love – ultimately, love of God. Developing a theme he found in **Plotinus,** Augustine gave an account of evil as a privation of good rather than understanding evil as a positive reality in itself. Thus, it is an error to attribute evil to God. His creation is not flawed or the result of less than perfect knowledge or power. Rather, we are to understand created beings as just that; beings who are (unlike God) less than perfect, though not defective through any defect in their creator. There is resonance of **Plato**'s doctrine of the degrees of reality – a normative hierarchy of being – in Augustine's thought. The freedom of human beings to act well or to act badly is a crucial part of theology and ethics. A deep concern with the nature of desire, **love,** and the peace of the virtuously ordered soul characterises Augustine's thought.

See **divine command theory, virtue**
Further reading: Augustine 1964 and 1998

Aurelius, Marcus (121–80 CE) Roman: **Stoic** thinker and Roman emperor from 161 CE. While engaged in the tasks of ruling, administration and warfare he still wrote on Stoic themes (*Meditations*). This work reflects many of the main (especially Roman) Stoic views, especially concerning self-command and the presence in man of a divine nature through which we may understand our selves and our place in the world.

See *ataraxia,* **Epictetus, natural law**
Further reading: Aurelius 1989

autonomy: There are several different notions of autonomy, including personal autonomy, moral autonomy and political autonomy. In different interpretations they have different relations to each other. Here we will focus on moral autonomy. In some moral theories (such as **Kant**'s), autonomy is of the first importance in that rational agents both formulate the moral law and are responsible for their actions. Both of these reflect their autonomy. In other theories (**Aristotle**'s is an example), self-determination is crucial, but not autonomy in the sense of self-legislation of an *a priori* principle of action.

In the more Kantian view, the morally autonomous agent is not only self-determining in acting but is also the author of moral principles. Conceptions of moral autonomy typically put a great deal of weight on connections between that authorship, moral agency, and rationality. They hold that autonomy is a condition for one to be morally responsible and a full-fledged moral agent. In Kant's view we are morally self-legislating and are motivated by our recognition of what our own reason requires. Autonomy has also been held to be a basis for self-respect and respecting others in that, if agents are autonomous, they are not to be treated or regarded merely as means for the interests and purposes of others. Kant's understanding of autonomy has roots in **Stoic** notions of self-mastery and acting in accord with one's rational nature. Autonomy as political liberty, having the freedom to pursue one's ends and interests with a minimum of interference, is a separate matter and is compatible with a number of approaches to morality that do not involve autonomy in the Kantian sense.

See **respect**

Further reading: Hill 1991; Kant 1976; Raz 1986

axiology: This is the philosophical study of value. Normative theory concerns moral requirements and substantive accounts of what is right and what is wrong, what is good and what is bad. Axiology is not directly concerned with normative issues, but with the nature and status of values. It addresses questions such as whether moral value is objective, whether value is found in states of affairs or in actions, the difference between intrinsic and extrinsic value, and whether value is an object of cognition.

Ayer, A. J. (1910–89) English: Ethics was not Ayer's primary area of philosophy but his articulation and defence of an emotivist account of ethical discourse in *Language, Truth and Logic* proved to be seminal. Defenders of **emotivism** went on to develop more sophisticated accounts and had the advantage of being able to respond to objections to emotivism, but Ayer's discussion remains an early, clear and polemically vigorous presentation of emotivism.

See **anti-realism, prescriptivism, Stevenson**
Further reading: Ayer 1952

benevolence: This is affective concern for the well-being of others. The benevolent person is moved to act with a view to the good of others out of a disposition of sensibility rather than strictly principled considerations. On some moral theories, benevolence is pointed to as a basis for moral concern that comes naturally to human beings and is as much a part of our nature as self-interest. In that sort of view, it needs only to be encouraged and extended, rather than somehow inculcated against the grain of natural selfishness. Benevolence in this broad sense has an important place in particular in the tradition of British moralists from the seventeenth century up to the nineteenth century. **Mill** appealed to it as a way of making the case for **utilitarianism,** and earlier, **Hume** and others appealed to it as part of the argument against Hobbesian **egoism.** It is possible for an agent to act with a view to the good of others without benevolence; one may see that certain actions are required even though one does not feel for the good of others. One could be **altruistic** on the basis of principles. That is something different from benevolence, which involves sensibility and motivation of a certain kind. Whether a certain sensibility is required for moral judgement and moral motivation is a long-standing issue.

Further reading: Hobbes 1991; Hume 1975 and 1978; Hutcheson 2002; Kant 1976; Mandeville 1924; Mill 1979; Smith 1984

Bentham, Jeremy (1748–1832) English: Bentham's writings are voluminous and they cover many areas. In moral theory he is best known for his conviction that there can be a **hedonic** calculus, a system for measuring **utility** in an empirical, objective way. This was to provide the instrument for assessing actions, practices and policies with a view to their efficacy in promoting **happiness**, understood as pleasure. Later utilitarians such as Mill distanced themselves from the hedonic calculus, finding it implausible and problematic in various respects. In particular, the issue of measurement and the issue of whether there are qualitative distinctions among pleasures raised serious objections to a strictly quantitative approach to assessing pleasure and thereby measuring utility. However, Bentham remains a key figure in the development of utilitarianism, and a key figure in the critique of **natural rights** and the social **contract**, both of which he took to be fictional and unhelpful to moral theory. In addition, his thought represents an important type of overall approach to moral theorising as the attempt to develop it as a kind of applied social science, a theoretical apparatus to be empirically applied and tested without reliance on custom, revelation, intuition or metaphysics. Bentham was interested in moral theorising for its practical application in policy and he was concerned with quite concrete issues in law, penology and rights. That commitment to genuine practical engagement had a powerful influence on utilitarians in succeeding generations.

See **consequentialism, monism, naturalism**
Further reading: Bentham 1996

Blackburn, Simon (1994–) English: He is a contemporary defender of **projectivism** whose roots he finds in **Hume**'s theorising. In his critique of moral **realism** he aims at showing its untenability and that projectivism does not weaken the authority of moral claims. He has elaborated a view in which morality has all of the form and genuineness that a realist would insist on, but without realist metaphysical commitments in respect of moral values. That is, he does not think morality is weakened in any fundamental way if there are no moral facts or objective values. In particular, he has been critical of realists' attempts to give an account of moral values as **supervening** on non-moral facts and properties. Blackburn argues that we should instead interpret values as supervening **projectively**. The moral features of situations and actions depend upon non-moral features, but they do so because of how we project values, not on account of values being **objective** features of the world. He has characterised his view as a version of **naturalism** in that he believes there are good naturalistic explanations for why human beings have the kinds of interests and sensibilities that underlie moral concern and commitment. There is a naturalistic account of why human beings have the sorts of concerns and propensities that can be developed into morality but moral value is not definable in terms of natural facts and properties. This is not realist naturalism, but a combination of naturalism and **expressivism**. Like Hume, Blackburn takes his view to be an account of morality, not an account of why there is no such thing. He calls his approach 'quasi-realism' because of how it retains the surface features of realist moral discourse without the metaphysical commitments that he regards as intractably problematic.

See **anti-realism, subjectivism**

Further reading: Blackburn 1993 and 1998

Bradley, Francis Herbert (1846–1924) English: Bradley wrote widely in philosophy and his destructive critique of **utilitarianism** has proved to be one of his chief contributions to ethics. He developed his critique of utilitarianism's conception of the moral agent and moral value from the standpoint of an idealist philosophy. According to Bradley's metaphysics reality is best understood as a coherent totality of thought rather than as a system of experiences or mind-independent objects. Bradley's main objections to utilitarianism were aimed at showing it to involve a falsifying conception of the moral agent as a separate individual ultimately seeking only pleasure. His critique of **hedonism** has had lasting influence, even for many who do not share his overall philosophical position. There was a period of great vitality of British idealism in the late nineteenth century and early twentieth century. The figures in that period developed important critiques of empiricism, **naturalism,** hedonism and utilitarianism. Bradley's essay, 'My Station and its Duties' was instrumental in broadening Anglo-American interest in Hegel's thought.

See **Green**

Further reading: Bradley 1876

Butler, Joseph (1692–1752) English: A moral theorist and theologian, best known in moral philosophy for his critique of ethical **egoism,** his conception of **conscience,** and his categorising of basic principles of action into

(a) particular passions or affections, (b) self-love, (c) **benevolence** and (d) conscience. Butler added that the last is the most authoritative (if not always the most powerful) and that a moral agent can find this out for herself in cool-headed reflection. The strength of even pressing desires and passions can be resisted by our grasp of what it is right to do, in contrast to what we feel affectively or appetitively urged to do. Butler explored central issues of moral psychology, moral epistemology and moral motivation. In his time debates about egoism and the relation of self-interest to **happiness** and to morality were prominent. He remains a figure of both historical and theoretical interest for his contributions to those debates.

See **Hobbes, Hume, Mandeville**
Further reading: Butler 1991

Cambridge Platonists: These were a group of Cambridge-educated seventeenth-century thinkers who came to have a good deal of influence on ethics and theology. What unified them as a group was the view that reason has a fundamental place in morality and that even God's ordering of value is rational; the good is good in itself and not because God wills it. They were much involved in theological disputes and made for a moderate party in contrast to the Calvinism they opposed, a faith in which divine **voluntarism** was crucial. In addition, they argued against the sort of voluntarism they found in **Hobbes**'s thinking. They were also opposed to empiricism insofar as it diminished the claims of reason. Some main figures among the Cambridge Platonists are **Ralph Cudworth,**

Henry More and Benjamin Whichcote. The movement was characterised by optimism in regard to the power of reason; opposition to religious enthusiasm; and embrace of the Platonic notions of the eternality and immutability of good, and the aspiration to attain true understanding and a justly harmonised soul.

See **Clarke, Plato**

Further reading: Cudworth 1991; Plato 1992

categorical imperative: In many theories moral requirements are held to be categorically imperative; that is, they are requirements that are unconditioned by an agent's interests or desires. **Kant** famously made the concept of the categorical imperative the centrepiece of his moral theory. In his view, moral requirements and only moral requirements are categorically imperative. Moreover, if there were no categorically imperative principles of action, there would be no genuine moral requirements. Moral duties alone express requirements on action that are based upon a principle of action that need not have a ground in the agent's desires or passions. Kant gave numerous formulations of the categorical imperative and held that they were equivalent. Perhaps the most frequently used formulation is, 'Act only according to that maxim by which you can at the same time will that it should become a universal law'. The imperative does not itself tell you what action to perform. It supplies a criterion for testing rules of action to see if they are morally valid. He argued that any account of morality that takes moral duties to be **hypothetically imperative** (imperative on a condition) would fail to reflect and respect what is essential in morality, namely, that its demands have an independent and overriding character. If the rationality of moral requirements or the motive to act upon them were conditional upon their expected contribution to some end (e.g. **happiness**) or if they depended upon the presence of some inclination (e.g. the sympathetic desire to relieve distress and improve the conditions of others) morality would be disfigured and undermined by depending upon factors and conditions external to it.

The Kantian worry is that in being thus dependent, the fulfilment of moral requirements would depend upon something non-moral and contingent. Through our awareness of ourselves as being able to respond to duty – the moral 'ought' – as well as to inclination, we recognise that there are indeed moral requirements commanded by reason, and that they reflect a distinctive kind of necessity. It is basic to Kant's theory that rationality alone enables us to recognise moral requirements and to respond to their normative authority.

The notion that moral requirements are categorically imperative figures in theories other than Kant's, though; sometimes in ways he would find objectionable. For instance, does **Aristotle**'s virtuous agent see that what is fine and just is categorically imperative for him? Perhaps yes, though, in becoming sufficiently virtuous to see that, the agent must develop certain desires and responses that enable him to read situations in that way. How agents recognise requirements as categorically imperative can depend upon the moral psychology the theorist finds most plausible, or vice versa.

See **deontology, virtue**
Further reading: Donagan 1977; Foot 1978 and 2001; Kant 1976; Korsgaard 1997; McDowell 1978

Clarke, Samuel (1675–1729) English: A theologian and moral philosopher, Clarke defended moral **realism** and a **rationalist** approach to ethics. In those respects he has a place in early modern **intuitionism** and **foundationalism**.
See **Cambridge Platonists**
Further reading: Clarke 1991

cognitivism: The cognitivist holds that moral knowledge is possible, and that the grounds for moral judgements are objective. It is incumbent upon the cognitivist to supply an account of what kinds of considerations those are, and how they can be known, but the key general commitment is a commitment to moral judgements as being evaluable in terms of truth and falsity. Moral statements are not to be interpreted only as expressing attitudes, conventions or personal endorsements. Moral claims are true or false by virtue of **objective** moral considerations. There is room for argument over whether they are true or not, and whether if true, they admit of exceptions.

There are several variants of cognitivism. Some are **naturalistic** (e.g. **Mill**), some are not. Some are **intuitionist** theories (**Moore**), some are not. Some are **virtue-centred theories** (e.g. **Aristotle**), others are not. Some (e.g. **Kant**) hold that moral judgements are ascertained to be correct or not according to use of an *a priori* principle. Cognitivism as such does not commit the theorist to a single, specific moral epistemology, though, of course, only those within a certain broad range will support cognitivism. Nor is cognitivism mapped onto specific positions on normative matters. Critics of cognitivism often emphasise two alleged difficulties for the view. One concerns the metaphysics of values. How can values be objective? How could there be such things as moral facts or objective moral properties? The other concerns the action-guiding features of moral considerations. How can the fact that 'X is right or obligatory' motivate an agent to do X? How could the fact that something is the case be prescriptive in itself? Surely desire or affect or some other non-cognitive aspect of our nature is necessary to account for (a) what we take to have moral value, and (b) the motivation to act on moral considerations. Cognitivism is closely related to **realism** and the terms are often used nearly interchangeably, but realism emphasises the metaphysics of moral value while cognitivism emphasises moral epistemology.

See **Ayer, Blackburn, emotivism, error theory, expressivism, Hume, Mackie, McDowell, non-cognitivism, non-naturalism, Plato**

Further reading: Aristotle 1985; Moore 1994; Plato 1992; Railton 1986; Ross 1930; Sturgeon 1988

coherentism: This is a view of epistemological justification. Coherentists argue that there are no foundational knowledge claims, and every belief or knowledge claim requires justificatory support from others. No knowledge claim is evident in itself or known to be true by **intuition**. Rather, justification is a matter of the degree of coherence of a claim within an overall system of claims (moral and non-moral) where coherence is a matter of explanatory and logical relations among the various claims. The more complete the coherence, the higher the degree of justification. Though rejecting **foundationalism**, coherentism is compatible with **cognitivism** and **objectivity**. There may be intuitive sources of moral beliefs, if by 'intuitive' we mean 'convictions that we hold firmly and regard as fundamental' but they still need coherentist justification. There is no necessary connection between coherentism and **subjectivity** or **relativism** – though it is consistent with them as well. **Rawls**'s strategy of **reflective equilibrium** is a prominent example of coherentism in moral epistemology.

Further reading: Brink 1989; Rawls 1971

commensurable: In recent decades there has been considerable debate over the question of whether values are commensurable. That is, can the values of different things be ordered by a single, common measure? Is the value of autonomy commensurable with the value of well-being? Is the value of friendship commensurable with the value of justice? And so forth. While much of the discussion of the issue concerns different sources of value, the issue can arise even when the values in question are of the same type, as in hedonic **utilitarianism**. For example, is one person's **happiness** commensurable with another person's? The issue of commensurability bears on fundamental questions concerning moral deliberation and the justification of moral decisions. It also bears on whether there are situations of unavoidable moral tragedy in the sense that even the most strongly justified course of action involves disvalue with which we must reconcile ourselves. Perhaps not all values are jointly realisable, and in some cases, there may be significant moral costs.

See **monism, pluralism**

Further reading: Nagel 1985; Raz 1986

conscience: Questions concerning the nature and role of conscience became prominent and central issues in moral theory through the Jewish and Christian traditions. In ancient Greek and Roman moral thought there are extensive discussions of self-knowledge, awareness of the moral features of one's actions and character, and the differences between **vice** and **weakness of will**. Conscience as morally authoritative has had a crucial role in morality influenced by theology, though it has also been taken up in completely secular ethical thought. There are several different interpretations of conscience. Among them are the following: (a) conscience as a faculty of moral cognition – a faculty that enables us to ascertain what is morally right and what is morally wrong (**Butler**); (b) conscience as a mode of developed sensibility such that we feel painful regret and remorse when we act contrary to it (**Mill**); (c) conscience as an internal judge of the moral worth of our ends and motives. Conscience does not determine what we are to do, but it can judge whether we have acted in a morally worthy manner (**Kant**); (d) conscience as faculty of practical reason by which we deliberate with a view to deciding on particular actions to perform, in aiming at conformity with moral principles. Conscience specifies particular actions in the overall project of aiming at what we take to be good. This allows scope for the possibility that an agent could be conscientious but have wrong values (**Aquinas**); (e) conscience as a reflective consideration guiding employment of criteria of moral soundness with a view to ascertaining which actions meet those criteria (**Smith**). Some of the main issues regarding conscience are (a) whether acting in accord with conscience renders one blameless, even if what one does is wrong; (b) whether it is morally worse to act contrary to conscience and be a hypocrite, or to act wrongly though conscientiously; (c) whether conscience is a faculty that is part of our nature or is acquired; (d) what the conditions are in which it is appropriate to disobey the law and legal authority when what they require is contrary to conscience; (e) by what tests we can determine whether conscience is a proper guide to action and moral self-evaluation.

Further reading: Aquinas 1998; Butler 1991; Kant 1976; Mill 1979; Smith 1984

consequentialism: A consequentialist theory holds that the locus of moral value is in the states of affairs brought about by actions or practices; that is, consequences are what morally matter. For the consequentialist, the central concern of moral evaluation is the difference that is made by actions, rather than the character of the agent, the character of the motive, or the action-type in itself. For example, if there are good reasons to regard deceitful promises as morally wrong, it is not simply because they are deceitful; it is because of the undesirable consequences of making such promises. If coming to the aid of those in distress is morally good, it is not simply because it reflects sympathetic concern; it is because people are better off as a result. Indeed, that is what makes sympathetic concern itself morally valuable. Perhaps the most familiar consequentialist theory is hedonistic **utilitarianism**, the theory that actions are to be evaluated on the basis of how much utility (interpreted as pleasure) they produce, or tend to produce.

Among the main issues faced by consequentialist theories are the following: (a) giving a satisfactory account of moral value that is fully independent of motive, the character of the agent, and action type. To many people it seems that some action-types are intrinsically right or intrinsically wrong, regardless of their consequences. This would have to be explained or explained away by consequentialism; (b) giving a satisfactory account of what features of consequences or what states of affairs morally matter – is it their desirability, the pleasure of them, or something else?; (c) responding to the concern that an agent may intend certain consequences while the action brings about others (e.g. can actions be subjectively right but objectively wrong?). Though it has antecedents going back much earlier, consequentialism has had a central place in moral theorising since the middle of the nineteenth century.

See **deontology, hedonism, Kant, Mill, non-consequentialism**

Further reading: Anscombe 1958; Mill 1979; Kant 1976; Scheffler 1982

contract theory: A contract theory explicates fundamental moral principles on the basis of an account of what rational agents would agree to. That is, we arrive at basic moral principles by ascertaining what rational agreement would converge upon, rather than appealing to principles independent of what agents would accept through a project of formulation rather than discovery. Contract theory highlights the fact that individuals who have different desires, interests and concerns nonetheless share certain fundamental interests and concerns. Those are the basis for fashioning a fair moral or political order, an order in which the basic rules and principles do not favour or disfavour anyone simply on account of what those rules and principles are.

The contractarian approach has been influential in both moral theory and political theory. **Hobbes, Locke** and **Rousseau** are key figures in the tradition. In their accounts, that starting position was the '**state of nature**'. Of course, what an agent will rationally accept and regard as endorsable depends on how such agents and their predicament are conceived. Hobbes was especially concerned with how to structure and sustain a just political order given that people compete for all manner of goods, differ in their views of important matters (such as religion) and have a natural right to defend themselves. Conflict is easily motivated by differences in interests and by concerns about security, and Hobbes was seeking a rationally compelling strategy for extricating rational agents from that basic condition. Locke was particularly concerned with the security of life, liberty and property if there was no institutionally regular, recognised juridical power. In those respects, Hobbes and Locke are figures of the first importance in early modern and modern theories of the state, state power, sovereignty and individual rights. Rousseau was articulating an approach intended to restore human freedom unadulterated by the corruptions of civilised life. The general methodology of the approach is to ascertain basic principles, rules and constraints that are universally agreeable and unforced, and thereby justified.

Contract theory can be seen as a rival to **consequential-ism** and **intuitionism** as strategies of justification. There has been a particularly close connection between con-tract theory and liberal political theory insofar as both are centrally concerned with the **rights** and liberties of in-dividuals and with what the proper powers and limits are on the power of the state. **Rawls** and Scanlon's works are notable and widely discussed contemporary examples of contract theory.

See **natural law, original position**

Further reading: Gauthier 1986; Hobbes 1991; Locke 1988; Rawls 1971 and 1997; Rousseau 1978; Scanlon 1997 and 2000

Cudworth, Ralph (1617–88) English: One of the **Cambridge Platonists,** Cudworth argued against divine **voluntarism** as the account of moral value. God wills only that which is good, but divine volition does not make its object good. The weight put on reason in Cudworth's epistemol-ogy, and his view of the metaphysics of the good, reflect **Platonic** themes. Cudworth's concern with the **Euthyphro problem** was motivated in part by what he took to be deficiencies in the more Calvinist conception of human nature as depraved, and our utter dependence upon the grace of God, whose will constitutes the good.

See **intuitionism**

Further reading: Cudworth 1991

deontology: This is one of the main approaches with regard to the structure of moral theory and its conception of the locus of moral value. In a deontological theory, duties (and correlatively, **rights**) are fundamental, in contrast to, say, consequences, intended outcomes, or the character of the agent. None of those is the central consideration for a deontologist. **Virtue** may still be regarded as important. For example, **Kant** took it to be quite important, but virtue will be explicated in terms the agent's acting dutifully, in that the agent is virtuous on account of a steady determination to do what duty requires. This is quite different from an **Aristotelian** or a **consequentialist** notion of virtue. In those approaches there is a conception of an end that is to be realised or brought about to the maximal extent, and that end and its value are the mooring to which the rest of the theory is tied. A deontological theory does not take an end or a state of affairs to be the key locus of moral value. It provides a certain sort of answer to the questions, 'To what do we look to find moral value'? and 'What is it that is the central concern of moral reasoning and decision'? The answer in both cases focuses on the theorist's conception of what are intrinsically right actions, and as such, actions it is one's duty to perform. It may be that doing X will have unhappy consequences for some agents, but the rightness of doing X can be ascertained independently of that. Indeed, the deontologist argues that it must be. The rightness of X is a feature of *it*, not of what it brings about. Moreover, agents' rights (or at least some of them) are fixed constraints on how others may permissibly treat them.

It should be noted that theories are rarely *purely* deontological; Kant included **happiness** in the 'sole and complete' good, though he argued that the good will is the highest good. Moreover, there are significant differences between versions of deontological morality. In **W. D. Ross**'s theory there are different kinds of duties resting on different kinds of bases. For example, there is a duty of non-maleficence (not harming) and it has a different basis from duties based upon previous acts of my own (for example, making amends for a wrong that I have committed). Kant argued that there is a single moral law even if it is susceptible to various formulations. Ross argued that we are cognisant of different duties and grounds of rightness through awareness of various features of actions. The morally relevant features of actions are of several kinds, and are not reducible to one type, principle or criterion. A theory need not be deontological in order to include the notion of duties or moral requirements. What distinguishes deontology is the account of the basis of duties and the way in which that shapes judgement and deliberation about what one is required to do.

See **intrinsic value, intuitionism, non-consequentialism, *prima facie*, virtue-centred theorising**

Further reading: Aristotle 1985; Donagan 1977; Kant 1976; Mill 1979; Ross 1930

divine command theory: This is the view that moral value, principles and moral obligation are grounded in divine will. Systematic reflection on this view goes back at least as far as **Plato**'s *Euthyphro*, and the central difficulty of the view remains much the same, that is, does God command what he commands because it is good (or right), or is the good (or the right) what it is just because God commands it? In Western monotheistic traditions it is widely held that God's commands are the basis of moral requirements, and that God is morally perfect. However, the question of the relation between being commanded and being morally right remains problematic. Also, while divine command theory is an approach that clearly gives moral commands enormous authority, there is the further issue of whether moral requirements need to be sanctioned and supported in that way in order to be authoritative for human beings. Why could we not be able to ascertain what is right, and be motivated to do it, just on the basis of our own reason and understanding? Moreover, what is the relation between our moral understanding and revelation? Are there elements of morality that could not be grasped by unaided reason? Even though divine command involves a supernatural being and its will, it can still be seen as a version of moral objectivism because of the status of moral principles. That is, they are objectively right *because* they are grounded in God's will. Of course, critics of theism will argue that the theistic basis of the approach is a reason for denying that it is form of objectivism.

See **Aquinas, Kant, Maimonides, natural law, Scotus, voluntarism, William of Ockham**

Further reading: Aquinas 1948; Geach 1969; Kant 1976; Maimonides 1956; Plato 1981; Quinn 1978; Scotus 1987; William of Ockham 1997

double effect, principle of: According to this principle, at least some actions that have both good and bad effects are permissible. They are permissible as long as the bad effects, though foreseeable, are not intended, and the good that is achieved is not achieved as a result of the bad effects. (The action that aims at a good end is not in itself a wrong action.) In war, for example, it is morally required that we (a) try not to harm civilians, and (b) not try to harm civilians. However, we may see that a certain attack, for which there is justification, will (undoubtedly but unintentionally) harm civilians. Killing civilians is not the means of defeating the enemy we are justified in attacking, in the cases in which we are justified in using deadly force. The issue of proportionality is also relevant. An action with potentially very significant foreseeable effects may not be justified if say, in the conduct of a military campaign, its tactical benefits are minor. However, attacking a target in such a way that civilian casualties can be foreseen may not be wrong in itself if it is justifiable as a crucial element in a morally valid attack on an unjust aggressor. The principle has been the focus of considerable controversy – both with respect to its formulation and with respect to its justification – especially in the context of the destruction of a foetus as part of a medical procedure, **euthanasia,** and other medical ethical issues.

Further reading: Aquinas 1998; Foot 1967; Grisez and Boyle 1979

E

egoism: Typically, a distinction is made between psychological egoism and ethical egoism. The former is a descriptive theory about how, in fact, people are motivated. It holds that people always and only act with a view to what they take to be their own self-interest. Ethical egoism is a normative theory, a theory about how people ought to act. It holds that agents ought to act only with a view to promoting their own self-interest. That is the fundamental principle of rational action. It is possible to endorse ethical egoism without also believing that psychological egoism is true. In that case, one would hold that agents are often not as self-interested as they rationally should be. If it is rational to act in a way that promotes the interests of others, doing so is rational and justified only if it is a means to promoting one's own interests. A somewhat weaker version is the view that we have no obligation to give moral weight to the interests and well-being of others. In either version **altruism** has no justification in its own right, Similarly, **virtues** such as honesty, loyalty, generosity, courage, fairness and many others *are* virtues only (argues the egoist) because of how they serve the end of maximising self-interest. Any form of them that did not do so would be a form that could not be considered virtuous. The non-egoist theorist argues that states of character that are excellent only because they promote self-interest could hardly be counted as virtues. For example, if friendships were altogether self-seeking, in what sense would either party's involvement in the relationship exhibit the loyalty, empathy, respect and concern that certainly seem to be crucial to genuine friendship? The ethical egoist and non-egoist interpret **prudence** differently. For the non-egoist it is not a narrow matter of self-interest but an understanding of human good. For the non-egoist virtuous activity is good for the virtuous agent, but it is good because it is virtuous, not simply because it serves the agent's interest.

See **benevolence, Hobbes, Mandeville**

Further reading: Butler 1991; Hobbes 1991; Hume 1975 and 1978; Mandeville 1924; Mill 1979

emotivism: This is the view that moral language has emotive meaning but not cognitive meaning. In this case there are no moral facts or objective moral considerations. Rather, there are non-moral facts and the attitudes toward them that are expressed in moral judgements. To say 'Kidnapping and blackmail are wrong' is to express a stance toward those actions – disapproval – but not to report or describe any objective moral features. We might find the action repugnant, but that is a response to it that we have, it is not a report of a feature of the action itself. If we say, 'Nearly everyone agrees that kidnapping and blackmail are wrong', we are reporting a factual matter and we can be literally correct or mistaken. But it is not a moral fact about those actions. Emotivists do not regard moral language as meaningless. Indeed, they take emotive meaning and its role (in expressing and influencing attitudes and responses, and so on) to be very important. The denial of meaning concerns cognitive meaning. Emotivists typically do not see themselves as 'attacking' or diminishing morality. Their view is intended to give an account of moral discourse.

The view was originally developed in a way that depended heavily upon certain empiricist criteria of meaning, though the endorsement of emotivism is not limited to Logical Positivists. **Hume**'s theory of morality is an important historical source for some elements of emotivism, at least with respect to kinds of theories being argued *against*. Hume's theorising involved a range of considerations and was not mainly driven by a specific criterion of empirical meaningfulness. He saw **intuitionists** and **rationalists** to be his chief opponents. Later on, emotivists saw themselves as taking on similar opponents. They agreed with **Moore** that **naturalism** is untenable, but they went in an **anti-realist**, rather than **realist** direction.

See **Ayer, Blackburn, objectivity, prescriptivism**
Further reading: Ayer 1952; Blackburn 1993 and 1998; Hume 1975 and 1978; Stevenson 1963

Epictetus (c. 55–135 CE) Greek: Born in Asia Minor, lived in Rome for a period, and was exiled. He was an influential teacher of **Stoicism**, especially as a moral philosophy and a guide to life. There is especially pronounced emphasis on self-command and responsibility for one's own character and actions in Epictetus's work.

See **Aurelius**, *ataraxia*
Further reading: Epictetus 1948

Epicurus (341–270 BCE) Greek: Epicurus developed a type of **hedonism** in which the exercise of **practical wisdom**

is central. The sustained tranquillity of mind sought by the practically wise person is the highest type of **happiness**. This tranquillity requires the person to recognise what merits concern, fear and desire, and what does not, in order to attain and sustain composure and calmness of mind. This is a hedonist conception of happiness, but not a vulgarly hedonist theory. Epicurus argued that pleasure is the good, but he did not regard this as a basis for simply seeking as many and as intense pleasures as possible. Rather, he regarded the absence of pain, and the removal of sources of pain (as in eating when hungry) as the most important pleasures. In that regard, much of the emphasis is on minimising pain and all the attendant frustration, agitation and longing that comes with being perturbed by desire. Epicurus's hedonism is as much a retreat from pain and its sources as it is a pursuit of pleasure. It involves distinguishing between natural pleasures and groundless ones, and also between necessary natural pleasures and unnecessary ones. The distinctions are an important part of the understanding one needs in order to seek what merits being sought. The desires, the satisfaction of which is needed for a pleasant and tranquil life, are not great in number and need not constantly agitate and make the pursuit of pleasure anxious and distracting. Later on, J. S. **Mill** defended a hedonist theory of value, and clearly felt the need to pre-empt the objection that a hedonist theory of value is base or ignoble, human beings being capable of much higher aspirations. Mill argued that Epicurus had already met this objection, though its persistence once again motivated replying to it.

See *ataraxia*

Further reading: Epicurus 1994; Mill 1979

error theory: This is a position on the status of moral claims. It holds that a key assumption of ordinary moral discourse – that it refers to objective values – is false, though not meaningless. Error theory was developed as a way of critiquing realism without denying that moral claims are cognitively meaningful. Emotivists and prescriptivists often argued that moral claims have only emotive meaning and not cognitive meaning because they do not refer to facts. Error theorists noted that moral discourse at least *seems* to be cognitively meaningful (and not only expressive) and that this feature requires explanation, even if it is found (as they claim it *is* found) that there are no objective values and that moral discourse makes an erroneous assumption. Thus, an error-theoretic approach holds that metaethical inquiry shows ordinary morality to involve a systematic misconception of its own character. Showing this is not entirely a matter of conceptual analysis or applying a specfic criterion of meaning, as is the case with emotivism. Rather, it is a result of a substantive examination of the assumptions of moral discourse, what is required in order for those assumptions to be fulfilled, and why people take such discourse to have the kinds of significance they attribute to it.

An error-theoretic approach can be taken in other areas of philosophical inquiry. For example, one might take that approach towards theism. Many people have beliefs about the existence and nature of God or gods, but (the argument goes) there is (or are) none. We need to explain why the belief persists, and may continue to do so, even though it is false. It is not simply a conceptual confusion or a matter of misused language. There is a substantive matter of belief at issue.

See **emotivism, Mackie, metaethics, prescriptivism**
Further reading: Mackie 1990

eudaimonism: '*Eudaimonia*' is often translated as 'happiness' or 'flourishing'. The eudaimonist holds that **happiness** or flourishing – a well-led life that the agent enjoys as such – is the proper basis for ethical theorising. Aristotle's ethics is a paradigmatic example of eudaimonism. Eudaimonists typically regard a conception of fully developed human nature or a fully actualised end proper to our nature, as the normative measure to apply to ethical issues. For instance, for **Aristotle**, the practically wise person, the agent who engages in virtuous activity, is best able to achieve *eudaimonia* through most fully actualising his nature as a rational animal. In many eudaimonistic theories there is an important connection between **virtue** and flourishing. The flourishing or happiness at issue is not interpreted simply as pleasure. This is not a version of **hedonism**. Rather, it is achieved through deliberate actions and seeking of ends guided by a correct understanding of human good. The activity is pleasing *because* it is caused by the proper operation of our rational capacities. It is pleasing because it is good, rather than the other way round. Thus, a conception of well-ordered human activity is the basis of living well, both in the sense of an excellent life and in the sense of a life that is enjoyed as worthwhile and free from regret over how one has exercised self-determination. (There may be grounds for regret concerning matters over which one had no control.)

Eudaimonia is different from *ataraxia*, though there are some affinities between the two. Both centrally involve rational self-determination, but the former involves it with a view to enjoying a number of key goods and fulfilled desires, and the latter involves it with a view to minimising the perturbance that desire can cause. It does this by regarding virtue, with respect to which we are understood as having full control, as the sole good, while eudaimonism includes other goods in its conception of value.

See **practical wisdom, prudence, virtue-centred theorising**

Further reading: Aquinas 1983; Aristotle 1985

euthanasia: In active euthanasia an agent intervenes to bring about someone's death in order to prevent the suffering that is making the subject's life miserable to the point of being unbearable. In passive euthanasia, means that are available to maintain life are either withheld or withdrawn. This leads to the death of the subject, though (as it is often argued) it is the underlying condition that causes death, rather than any person as an agent. In both kinds of cases what is at issue is whether it is morally permissible to take or withhold measures such that the death of the subject is intended (active euthanasia) or the death is foreseen, though not intended (passive euthanasia). If someone is suffering in an unendurable way and has no prospect of recovery or relief from suffering, the question of whether to continue treatment and/or the maintenance of life can loom very large. Defenders of passive euthanasia (but not active euthanasia) often argue that if there is sufficient evidence of the subject's approval, either from the subject himself or from a suitable proxy, of the withholding or withdrawing of treatment, it is morally permissible, and it does not constitute killing (no less, *wrongful* killing). **Utilitarians** often argue that objections to euthanasia (active and passive) are irrational impediments to alleviating avoidable suffering. Moreover, if the agent's consent supplies the assurance that we are doing what the patient most wants, we can be sure that this would not be wrongful killing.

See **Singer**

Further reading: Foot 1967; Rachels 1986; Singer 1981 and 1993

Euthyphro problem: In Plato's dialogue, *Euthyphro* (named for a figure in the dialogue), a basic dilemma concerning value is formulated. The interlocutors discuss the issue of whether what is pious is so because it is beloved by the gods, or whether the gods love those things because they are pious. This is the question of the ground or source of value. Is it intrinsic to things that are valued, or is it dependent upon being valued by, for example, God (gods) or human beings? This is a long-standing issue of the metaphysics of value, the question of value's most basic status, and whether *valuing* is the ground of value or not. Views that hold that valuing is the ground of value are **voluntarist** conceptions.

Under the heading 'voluntarist' are such disparate views as **emotivism, existentialism,** and some theistic conceptions (e.g. that of **William of Ockham**). The issue is acute for theists because it goes right to the heart of the question of the extent of God's freedom in willing and commanding with regard to value. If it were willed by God to be good, would it really *be* good to kill anyone over thirty who is not a parent? Or, on the secular plane, can something be good or right because of human volition or choice? In addition to this question about the ground of value, there is the issue of whether voluntarism can provide any tenable account of value because in that view, whatever is willed or chosen to be good, is good just for that reason. What resources are there in that view to show that valuation is anything but arbitrary given that there are no considerations to appeal to except the fact that X is valued? On the other hand, there are important and persistent difficulties with regard to how value as a reality independent of will and choice, is to be conceived. If it is independent of the will or desire or choice, what kind of ground could it have? How is it related to what does not have value? How do we attain knowledge of it? How does (or could) that knowledge be action-guiding and have any motivational efficacy?

See **Cudworth, expressivism, metaethics, Moore**

Further reading: Adams 1979; Cudworth 1991; Plato 1981; William of Ockham 1997

evolutionary ethics: This is a heading under which fall a number of approaches to ethical theorising all of which regard facts about biological evolution and natural selection as crucial to understanding moral values and moral behaviour. Many nineteenth-century versions of Social Darwinism used facts about natural selection as bases for holding that competitive behaviours and even aggressive behaviours have a ground in nature that justifies the ascendance of the strong over the weak. Theses of these types were applied both to individuals and to groups, such as nations or races (according to the prevailing understanding at that time). It should be noted, however, that in the nineteenth century T. H. Huxley, a strong champion of Darwin's theory, argued that while evolution by natural selection can explain how human beings came to have the propensities and susceptibilities that are the bases for morally relevant behaviours and feelings, questions of what is morally right and wrong are questions for moral thought in its own terms, and cannot be defined in terms of facts of nature.

In more recent decades, evolutionary ethics has taken into account developments in genetics and molecular biology, and their significance with regard to the understanding of **altruistic** behaviour and kin-selection. In conjunction with the discrediting of various more or less horrifying eugenics policies, these developments have led to a more scientifically respectable and conceptually sophisticated range of theories of evolutionary ethics. Issues concerning the unit of selection, the relation of genotype to phenotype and to behaviours, and questions about what are the relevant criteria and measures of success are receiving steadily closer and empirically informed attention. In recent years much of the controversy concerning evolutionary ethics has been focused on claims made on behalf of **sociobiology** and whether sociobiology can explain or justify various moral matters. Sociobiologists are often accused of making inflated and unsubstantiated claims about the extent to which biology accounts for morality. In general, evolutionary ethics is one type of ethical **naturalism**.

Further reading: Huxley 1989; Ruse 1986; Wilson 1978

existentialism: Existentialist thinkers reject the view that there is a rationally intelligible order of things such that basic moral values can be understood in terms of that order. For example, they reject the **Aristotelian** view that there is an end intrinsic to human nature and that rational activity can enable us to actualise that end. They also reject the **Kantian** view that there is an *a priori* principle (or any rational principle) that is a universal and adequate criterion of right action. They reject **naturalistic** and **non-naturalistic** realism across the whole spectrum, ranging from sociobiology to **Platonism**. Existentialism has had a considerable presence in Continental philosophy and a lesser presence in Anglo-American thought. However, at a very general level, there are some likenesses between some versions of **expressivism** and some existentialist views. The main point of contact is their shared rejection of **cognitivism** and **realism** and the way in which both approaches put a great deal of weight on stances and decisions rather than on moral knowledge or rationally required principles.

There are several different currents of existentialism, some with sources in **Nietzsche**, others with sources in **Kierkegaard**, **Sartre**, and Heidegger, among others. Some of them include theistic commitments while others are explicitly atheistic. They involve different conceptions of the setting and the role of radical choice (choice that is not governed by empirical considerations or rational principles) in valuing and in leading a life. Existentialist thinkers often put a great deal of weight on coming to grips with contingency and with human freedom. These are crucial because they maintain that we cannot find guidance for how to live by a comprehension of the world order. Human freedom, the anxiety as a result of freedom lacking objective ends or purposes, and the necessity to make ultimate choices are key elements of many existentialist thinkers's views of ethics. In that regard, existentialist ethics is a version of **voluntarism**. Commitment, and authenticity – taking responsibility for one's choices and values – are focal concerns for most existentialists.

See **Euthyphro problem, Murdoch**

Further reading: Kierkegaard 1946; Nietzsche 1966 and 1998; Sartre 1947

expressivism: This is a view about the status and meaning of moral claims. Expressivists hold that moral claims do not assert or report moral facts or beliefs; they are not to be interpreted in **cognitivist** terms. Rather, they are to be interpreted as expressing attitudes or stances. Moral claims are not literally true or false. The expressivist need not hold that the view weakens the significance of moral issues or claims about them. The expressivist can argue that moral issues have all the weight that we ordinarily take them to have, and that moral considerations and disagreements are to be taken seriously. However, moral convictions and judgements are not correct or incorrect in an objectively ascertainable manner. There are no moral facts or properties that are 'built into' the world as possible objects of cognition or perception.

There are numerous versions of expressivism, ranging from Ayer's **emotivism,** to more complex approaches such as **Hume's** and **Smith's**. Some expressivists emphasise the role of choice or decision with respect to moral values while others focus on moral discourse and its alleged lack of cognitive meaning and the way in which allegedly objective moral considerations are deeply problematic.

See **anti-realism, Ayer, Blackburn, existentialism, Hare, Mackie, naturalism, non-cognitivism, projectivism, realism, supervenience**

Further reading: Ayer 1952; Blackburn 1993 and 1998; Hare 1963 and 1973; Hume 1975 and 1978; Mackie 1990; Smith 1984

externalism: This is a view on the issue of moral motivation. An externalist denies that moral considerations simply as such have motivational efficacy. Thus, an agent could recognise that x, y and z are reasons for believing that action A is morally required, but that recognition in itself may not move the agent to do A. The motive is 'external' to what explains the moral status of the action (being obligatory, wrong, impermissible, and so on). Externalism takes the issue of what accounts for moral quality and the issue of what moves an agent to respond to moral quality to be distinct issues. Like **internalism**, it cuts across numerous other distinctions (such as **consequentialism/non-consequentialism, cognitivism/non-cognitivism,** hedonism/non-hedonism). However, there is more scope for a cognitivist to be an externalist because what leads some theorists to be non-cognitivists is the insistence that moral considerations must be practical, must have motivational efficacy. For that reason, theories in which moral value is grounded in affect, sensibility or desire have special appeal to non-cognitivists because that grounding can also explain why people are moved to act on their moral views and responses. If it is one's disapproval that is the basis for judging an action to be wrong, that disapproval is likely to have motivational force as well. We are 'against' acts of that kind.

Mill is an example of an externalist, that is, one who denies that there is an internal connection between moral considerations and moral motivation. In *Utilitarianism* he is quite clear about there being a difference between considerations about utility on the one hand, and the actual motivating factors that move people to act in accord with those considerations. On the other hand, **Kant** is a **rationalist** internalist holding that the recognition of an action as morally required supplies a rational motive for the agent to perform the action. There is also the Socratic view that knowledge of the good motivates an agent and that any source of motivation other than knowledge is not necessary for virtuous action. He held that no one does wrong actions voluntarily. They are always the result of ignorance. With knowledge, the agent would not have acted wrongly. In Aristotle's theory the agent with sound character is moved to do what virtue requires through both seeing that it is right and wanting to act virtuously. The weak agent or less firmly virtuous agent is someone in whom there is not that congruence of understanding and desire. Because he explicates the moral psychology in this way, there is no simple answer to the question of whether **Aristotle** was an internalist or an externalist. Perhaps we should say that for the virtuous agent moral motivation is of an internalist character.

See **Plato**

Further reading: Kant 1976; Mill 1979; Nagel 1970

F

Foot, Philippa (1920–): A key figure in **metaethical** debates in the last half-century, and an important figure in reviving interest in **virtue-centred ethical theorising**. Her work reflected a strong Aristotelian influence (both from

Aristotle and also **Thomas Aquinas**) though it was not an attempt to restate or defend Aristotle in a doctrinal sense. Foot argued that **non-cognitivists'** distinctions between (a) fact and value, and (b) descriptive meaning and **prescriptive** meaning misrepresented the elements of moral thought and motivation. She argued that it is implausible that a set of facts (e.g. without provocation a person severely beats another, and takes pleasure in administering the beating) has no ethical significance independent of whatever attitudes or responses we have toward those facts. In the judgement that beatings of that sort are wrong, we do not find two distinct elements, one of them descriptive (factual) and the other one prescriptive (evaluative). Not to recognise that the action as described is *wrong* is to fail to understand fully the concepts that apply to the action. Understanding that it is wrong is not a separate, non-cognitive issue of projecting our feelings or prescribing a rule for acts of that type. How we appreciate morally relevant considerations, and how they figure in moving us to act, depends upon dispositions of attention, receptivity and modes of deliberation that have become firmly established in us (for better or worse). Excellent dispositions are virtues, and bad dispositions are vices. There are **naturalistic** grounds for explicating human goods and also vices and virtues. In her more recent work she has enlarged upon her earlier treatment of the relations between practical rationality, human good and happiness.

See **Anscombe, cognitivism, emotivism, expressivism, Hare, projectivism, virtue**

Further reading: Foot 1978 and 2001

fortune: Since antiquity, moral theorists have been concerned with the way in which things we cannot control figure in our lives and in the moral quality of our actions and characters. This was of central concern to **Socrates, Aristotle**

and the **Stoics,** in large part because of the role they assigned to rational self-mastery in the well-led life. What difference (if any) should be made in our estimation of an agent if he has good luck with regard to both nature and society? If the person has a temperament well suited to acquiring the virtues, and is surrounded by morally sound and concerned agents does that make their virtue less praiseworthy? If we act from worthy motives but things go badly, what sort of criticism of us as agents is appropriate? Much ancient ethical thought raised a question that is still with us: Is it better to be virtuous through a struggle against inclination and bad habits, or is it better to have good luck that eases the acquisition of virtue? Is the relevant notion of 'better' a moral notion, or do we mean that it is better (in a non-moral sense) to have good luck but there is more *moral* virtue in prevailing against weakness and inclination? The importance of fortune is certainly not confined to antiquity. Wherever a theorist 'locates' moral value – in consequences, intentions, actions or character – there will be factors other than agency that are unavoidable. It is clear that we do not have full control over the outcomes of our actions, and even if we try to obviate that difficulty by putting weight on intentions, those too are formed in ways we do not entirely control. Our propensities and temperament, and thus, our ability to acquire excellent character, are influenced by natural and social factors. The issue of fortune, or '**moral luck**' as it is sometimes called, is motivated by the perplexities and difficulties raised by such considerations. Perhaps we are to strive for virtue, but our ability to do so is influenced by fortune. Perhaps we are to act autonomously, but it may be impossible to make a clean break between rational agency and other elements of our nature.

Kant's moral philosophy is an attempt to minimise the moral relevance of fortune, by locating moral value in the will, understood as a faculty of reason that operates independently of any conditions except a law of its own making. In that regard, his view has Stoic resonance. In regard to specific moral issues, punishment is a good example of the weight and importance of considerations of fortune. Two actions, exactly alike, except that in one the poison is strong enough to cause death, and in the other, it sickens but does not kill the victim, differ as crimes. The first is murder and the second simply is not. Supposing that to be a matter of fortune, are the two crimes equally grave? Do they merit the same punishment? Is an agent who has a volatile temper or has strong passions less than fully responsible for acting violently or impetuously? Is a person who has been habituated by corrupt people less responsible for becoming like them, rather than becoming virtuous or at least morally decent? Even where theorists do not raise the issue of fortune or moral luck using precisely that terminology, the issues are often discussed and their significance recognised.

Further reading: Aristotle 1985; Kant 1976; Mill 1979; Nagel 1985; Smith 1984; Statman 1993; Williams 1981

foundationalism: This is a position in epistemology that holds that there are basic or foundational knowledge claims, claims known to be true without requiring support by other claims. Foundational claims are justified through being self-evident. This does not mean that they are obviously true. It may be that experience and careful consideration are needed in order for a person to comprehend a foundational belief as self-evident. But it is justified through being evident in its own right. Foundational beliefs are uninferred basic beliefs that are parts of the justification of all other beliefs, namely, all those that are not known through self-evidence. **Intuitionism** in moral theory is the position that there are foundational moral beliefs. In the elaboration of his intuitionist moral epistemology **W. D. Ross** explicitly addressed the issue of some moral claims being self-evident but not obviously true.

See **Clarke, coherentism, Moore, Prichard, Reid**

Further reading: Brink 1989; Clarke 1991; Moore 1994; Prichard 1912; Ross 1930

G

greatest happiness principle: **Mill** and **Bentham** both use the expression 'greatest **happiness** principle' to refer to the main principle of **utilitarianism**. It is certainly most familiar in that usage. It is understood as the principle that those actions are right that promote the greatest happiness of the greatest number. In fact, **Francis Hutcheson** had earlier used the formulation that morally right action 'procures the greatest happiness for the greatest numbers' in *An Inquiry into the Original of our Ideas of Beauty and Virtue*. His use of the principle is somewhat different from that of the utilitarians, and his moral theorising overall has aesthetic elements foreign to classical utilitarianism. There is extensive recent discussion of the principle, and this includes some debate over whether the principle is coherent. One line of criticism is that it demands maximising in two ways, and the attempt to do so may put us in a predicament that cannot be resolved by any application of the principle. Compare a situation in which each person has a moderate and equal amount of utility to a situation in which a minority has a great deal of utility, and the majority has some, but not nearly as much. Which state of affairs more fully satisfies the principle? Regardless, the principle has been and remains an important central conception of a great deal of **consequentialist** moral theory.

Further reading: Bentham 1996; Hutcheson 2002; Mill 1979

Green, Thomas Hill (1836–82) English: Like other British idealists, such as **Bradley**, Green was a critic of moral theories that grounded action in passions, and that regarded moral agents as distinct individuals independent of larger social wholes. Green held that individuals are aspects of a rationally ordered whole comprising reality. This view reflects his absolute idealism and its rejection of atomic individualism, empiricism and **utilitarianism**.

Further reading: Bradley 1876; Green 1883

Grotius, Hugo (1583–1645) Dutch: Grotius wrote quite widely. (He wrote theology and poetry as well as more clearly philosophical works.) His greatest impact has been in philosophy of law and political philosophy. His works shaped key early modern notions of **natural law**, international law, and the basis of political obligation. He argued that natural law does not contradict fundamental (Judeo-Christian) revealed law, but also that the former has standing of its own and does not depend upon a divine source or sanction. He was particularly concerned to show how law properly constrains the conduct of warfare – that warfare need not be a wholesale suspension of morality and that considerations of **rights** and duties provide rules of normative governance for warfare. A key argument in his *On the Law of War and Peace* (*De Jure Belli ac Pacis*) holds that a right of self-preservation is basic to morality and that civil society's most fundamental task is to secure this **natural right**, making it possible for individuals to pursue their own interests. His focus on the naturalness of the right of self-preservation, the relation of the basis of political obedience to securing that right, and the way in which the right of self-protection (through the use of force) is taken up by the state, has had an impact on a great deal of theorising since his time.

In recent years, interest in Grotius has been increasing. The importance of his work for the treatment of issues concerning relations between religious and political power, and concerning religious tolerance is attracting renewed attention. He himself was an advocate of religious tolerance in large part because of its good effects with regard to unforced and sustainable political unity.

Further reading: Grotius 2004

happiness: Because of the evident interest in happiness that human beings have, it is a central issue in a great deal of moral theorising. It is often taken to have important connections with pleasure, **virtue**, self-interest and other fundamental moral concerns. In some theories (e.g. the **utilitarianism** of **Bentham** and **Mill**) it is interpreted in terms of pleasure on the grounds that pleasure is what we desire for its own sake and only for its own sake. In other theories (such as the **eudaimonism** of **Aristotle**) it is interpreted in terms of virtuous activity, and thereby connected to the excellences proper to a being with a rational nature. Aristotle argued that there are excellent activities that are pleasing because they are good, rather than the other way round, and that a life shaped by those activities is a happy life, happiness being the final end at which we aim. A well-led life, a life of excellent activity is a happy life, though pleasure is not the main end of life.

Even though he argued that happiness and the desire for it could not supply the basis for moral duties, **Kant** acknowledged the importance of happiness. He held that human beings, by nature, do indeed all desire happiness; it is not an optional end. Because by nature we all have inclinations, and cannot fail to have them, it is rational to desire happiness. Kant also argued that an additional reason to pursue happiness is that unhappiness can easily have a corrupting influence on our moral motivation. Frustration, resentment, anger at our situation can easily be turned into motives for action that take us in morally wrong directions. In order to increase the prospect of engaging in morally worthy action, we should strive to succeed at pursuing happiness. One other feature of Kant's view is that the complete good is happiness in accord with moral worth or virtue. That is the sort of just distribution of happiness that we cannot attain in our lives, but which is a moral ideal that God can realise.

In other approaches, such as **Stoicism**, happiness plays a less crucial role, at least if we take pleasure to be an essential element or feature of happiness. Stoics argued that what we should aim at is a kind of tranquillity in which we are undisturbed by passions and desires. This is what they took *ataraxia* to be. It is a kind of rational self-command that is more a matter of knowing what is worth caring about than it is a matter of successfully satisfying one's desires. This tranquillity can be interpreted as a Stoic version of happiness as long as the contrast between it and the other views is understood. The difference between achieving gratification – satisfying our desires; and being at peace because desires do not perturb us – is of the first importance.

In modern moral theorising a crucial distinction is often made between self-interest, **prudential** considerations (in a narrow construal of 'prudential') and moral or

altruistic considerations. In this approach, one of the key tasks of moral theory is to show why an agent would or should take altruistic considerations to be effectively action-guiding; why an agent would have practical concern for the interests and welfare of others. Self-interest is not necessarily the same thing as happiness, but there are obvious respects in which they are related. In antiquity, the contrast between self-interest and altruism was not drawn as sharply. Instead, the key issue for many thinkers was the distinction between real and apparent goods, or between the noble and the base.

In theistic conceptions of morality there is often a distinction drawn between naturalistic happiness and perfect happiness or beatitude. The latter essentially involves union with God, often interpreted as complete, continuous contemplation of God. In the views of key thinkers such as **Maimonides** and **Aquinas**, the happiness they regarded as the most complete and perfect is of that kind. This reflects an intellectualist ideal for human beings. It is because we possess intellect that we can be happy. This view has a background in Aristotle, who held that we are capable of happiness because we have a divine element in us (intellect). In Aristotle's view it is not that there is divine happiness, human happiness, and infra-human happiness. Rather, there is happiness, which the gods enjoy, and which we can enjoy to the extent that our intellect is actualised. In the religious tradition the most perfect happiness is loving union with God.

See **egoism, hedonism**

Further reading: Aquinas 1983; Aristotle 1985; Kant 1976; Mill 1979

Hare, Richard M. (1919–2002) English: Hare's critique of ethical **naturalism** and his development and articulation of **prescriptivism** have had a significant impact in metaethics during the last half-century. Through his examination of moral discourse and moral judgements he sought to show that moral naturalism is untenable. This is because it cannot explain the valuative, action-guiding dimension of moral claims. He also argued that though there are no moral facts there is a rational structure to moral judgements, and there are distinctive features of moral discourse. It is not to be interpreted in thinly **emotivist** terms. A key feature of morality is that moral claims, as expressive of moral judgements, are imperatives meant to apply **universally**. That is a key feature that distinguishes them from non-moral valuations, such as judgements of taste. We do not make moral claims intending them to refer only locally or within this or that specific group or community. Hare argued that though they are **non-cognitive**, they are not immune to critical examination or unsusceptible to rigorous formulation. His prescriptivism helped reintroduce considerations of rational structure into moral thought that was nonetheless **expressivist** in its conception of moral value. Hare's work had a great deal of influence on debates about the semantics of moral language, and also on the relation between facts and values.

See **supervenience, Foot**
Further reading: Hare 1963 and 1973

hedonism: A theory of value that maintains that pleasure is the good and is the ultimate end of action. There are several different versions of hedonism. In some versions, distinctions are made between higher and lower pleasures. That is, there are qualitative distinctions as well as quantitative distinctions. Defenders of hedonism are often anxious to avoid the charge of being 'vulgar' hedonists and propounding a view that barely distinguishes human ends and concerns from those of lesser creatures. However, hedonism as such is not vulgar or base. Whether it is or is not depends upon more specific features of the view as developed by the theorist. Pleasure and its relation to moral value is a central concern of many moral theories. For example, **Kant** understood it to be essential to **happiness,** and he regarded happiness in proportion to virtue as the complete good. But that does not introduce hedonism into his theory. According to Kant, the value of pleasure is not itself moral value, and there is something morally defective about a situation in which people are not happy in proportion to their moral virtue. **Aristotle** held that virtuous activity is pleasing, and that its pleasures are integral to happiness. But neither is that view an accommodation of hedonism. According to non-hedonists, pleasure may be a good, but it is not *the* good, nor is it necessarily morally valuable.

See **axiology, Bentham, Butler, Epicurus, eudaimonism, Mill, naturalism, virtue**

Further reading: Aristotle 1985; Bentham 1996; Butler 1991; Epicurus 1994; Kant 1976; Mill 1979

Hegel, G. W. F. (1770–1831) German: Hegel developed a systematic philosophy of absolute idealism; this is an idealism in which the world is understood as constituted by objective thought. There is no conception of reality independent from thought. However, the thought in question is not the subjective thought or experience of individuals, but the increasingly integrated totality of thought that is realised through history. Hegel was anxious to connect more fully or even equate the objective order with rationality, and this required abandoning **Kant**'s transcendental idealism, which posited things-in-themselves independent of mind and reason. In ethics, the departure from Kant was motivated by objections to Kant's theory as implausibly abstract and formal. According to Hegel, reason is present in social practices and it is reflected in concrete roles, responsibilities, and habits of action. It is not a criterion or measure separate from such things and it cannot rule actions in or rule them out according to a formal test. That approach is **subjective** in just the way Hegel thought that reason and ethics are not subjective. Through ethical life, through deliberate, voluntary action in the complex circumstances of concrete situations, value or good is realised, and it is realised in ways that are enactments of the agent's rational nature. It is through acting that one's subjectivity is externalised. A rational world order is constituted by self-determined rational activity and does not simply answer to an ideal principle for organising it (such as Kant's **categorical imperative**). This is why ethical activity involves both the free, rational activity of the subject and the duties, responsibilities, and normative constraints of an order in which the individual is a participant. Ethical life is both a realisation of freedom and law-governed. This conception relocates the ethical agent in a concrete, highly determinate objective order, in contrast to the Kantian conception, while affirming that activity in that order expresses the agent's freedom as a rational agent. This is Hegel's way of uniting the universal (the overall order of duties and obligations) with the particular (the individual rational agent).

Some recognisably Aristotelian influences are detectable in Hegel's ethical theorising even though his idiom is very different from Aristotle's and the philosophical context was quite different. (**Aristotle** had **Plato, Socrates,** and numerous **Sophists** in mind in developing his ideas. Hegel was motivated in part by Kant and other German idealists.) In the latter decades of the nineteenth century and the early decades of the twentieth century several British Idealist philosophers influenced by Hegel produced important works on ethics and politics. As with

Hegel himself, these thinkers developed conceptions and explanations of specific issues in ethics and politics on the basis of an overall metaphysical system of which ethics and politics were crucial elements. For it is in ethical activity and political life that the freedom and aspirations of rational agents are enacted and realised. At the same time that these theorists engaged in highly abstract metaphysical theorising, the emphasis that Hegel placed on the rationality of concrete practices and institutions is evident. Hegelian ethics, in its British legacy, had a clear concern with actual social life and the practical dimensions of social policy.

See **Bradley, Green**

Further reading: Hegel 1981

Hobbes, Thomas (1588–1679) English: Hobbes wrote widely in philosophy but is best known for *Leviathan*, one of his works focusing on politics, but with extensive treatment of related matters including human action, motivation, moral psychology, human nature and thought and judgement. Hobbes was a **natural law** theorist and gave an account of political authority and obedience based upon a conception of a social contract by which individuals surrender natural liberty for the security of the civil condition with a single, undivided sovereign. He has been interpreted by some as defending **egoism** as a theory of motivation, and political absolutism – a conception in which the sovereign power (perhaps even an individual king or ruler) has total power over the state and individuals' lives. At the same time, he has been interpreted as an important figure in the development of classical liberalism. This is because his conception of politics is one in which individual security is of paramount importance, and conceptions of good – the kinds of conceptions in accordance with which individuals lead their lives – are left to individuals as long as they do not upset or threaten the stability of the civil order. In that respect, Hobbes can be seen as trying to make room for diversity in conceptions of good. In his view, what each person pursues and their reasons why, are their own business. It is the business of the state to provide a stable order in which those pursuits are possible. If people are willing to give up their natural liberty and **rights** (the exercise of which in the state of nature makes for a precarious and conflict-ridden condition) in a social **contract** that creates a sovereign to rule a political order, then the advantages of the security that it provides will make it possible for people to lead their own lives in their own ways. Under this interpretation, Hobbes's sovereign looks less like a menacing absolute monarch and more like the kind of sovereign needed in a society in which there are diverse conceptions of good.

Hobbes's placing of religious authority in the political sovereign has also elicited quite different interpretations. On the one hand, it appears to be a strengthening of the sovereign's total control over society. On the other, it is seen as a way of making sure that society is not torn by allegiances to distinct authorities, and ensuring that ecclesiastical power does not compete with political authority. Seen from that perspective, Hobbes secularised religious power, rather than sacralising political power. Under any interpretation, Hobbes made a case for political order and the state being an artifact, created by rational agents, to meet their needs and interests. This notion of the state as an artifact, fashioned to protect the interests of individuals, marks a key development in early modern political thought. One difference between Hobbes and **Locke** and some other natural law theorists is that according to Hobbes, there is no **justice** or injustice in the **state of nature**. There is natural law and **natural right**, but justice and injustice depend upon the will of the sovereign. In the absence of a sovereign there is no authority to maintain or impose justice.

Further reading: Gauthier 1986; Hobbes 1991

Hume, David (1711–76) Scottish: He was the most influential of the British Moralists of the Enlightenment period, in ethics and in other areas of philosophy. In moral philosophy Hume argued against **rationalism** and against those who held that we have a distinctive **moral sense** that enables us to detect (and respond to) moral properties. He was a **sceptic** and a **subjectivist** about the status of values. He held that values are not **objective** features of, or entities in, the world and that they have their ground in human sensibility. But he did not believe that 'anything goes' in respect of morality, or that values are subjective in the sense of being simply a matter of personal choice or preference. He argued that there is a common basis for certain sentiments fundamental to morality and that concern for others as well as for ourselves is natural. It is not something one has to be argued into. In describing this common basis in sensibility he referred to what he called 'the *party* of humankind'. Hume was not a sceptic about the genuineness of morality; he was a sceptic with regard to the independent existence of moral values. He famously raised the question about the relation between what *is* and what *ought to be* or *ought to be done*. He also famously argued that reason is the slave of the passions. Reason cannot move us to act on its own, nor can it detect or construct moral value on its own. The passions are the ground for both value and motivation. Factual beliefs have a role in moral evaluation and deliberation, but there are no moral facts as possible objects of cognition. His subjectivist account sought to explain morality, including moral judgement, moral concern, and **virtue** and **vice** without reference to objective values, and without diminishing the reality and significance of morality.

His works comprise extensive discussions of how agents regard themselves and others, and the respective roles of what is found agreeable and what is found useful in accounting for fundamental elements of ethics. He gave an account of the origin and significance of **justice** in terms of human sentiments and **utility**. Because of the role of what he refers to as 'utility' in his theorising he has been regarded by some as a precursor to the classical utilitarianism of the nineteenth century, though he does not elaborate a normative account in the manner of the utilitarians. Hume's focus was more a matter of reflecting upon familiar moral phenomena and phenomenology, and seeking to account for them on the basis of sensibility, than a matter of providing an account of one or another criterion of right action.

His anti-**rationalism** and subjectivism were later on deployed in various ways by numerous thinkers, ranging from exponents of early forms of **emotivism** to current forms of **projectivism**. Hume's thought remains highly influential in recent metaethical debates concerning moral epistemology, the ontology of values, and the nature of moral motivation.

See **metaethics, Reid**

Further reading: Hume 1975 and 1978

Hutcheson, Francis (1694–1746) Irish (of Scots ancestry): Hutcheson's conception of the **moral sense** gave an integrated account of moral epistemology and moral approval and disapproval. Hutcheson was responding to theorists (such as **Samuel Clarke**) who held that moral judgement is a matter of reason discerning a relation of fitness, for example showing gratitude to a benefactor is a relation between persons, and it is a fitting relation, and as such, a virtuous one. Hutcheson held that moral properties are not relations, and therefore, they are not discerned by reason. Moral judgements do indeed have objects, and the judgements are true or false. They are, though, the work of a moral sense rather than reason. Grounding moral judgement in a moral sense (rather than in reason) enables us to give a better account of why we regard certain actions as virtuous, he thought. It is because we find them pleasing in a disinterested way. In considering a **benevolent** act we both perceive the **virtue** of it and we approve of it. The moral sense gives us access to the moral quality of acts and it is that through which we approve or disapprove of them. Moral sense is neither a matter of reason nor a matter of will. It operates independently of volition.

Hutcheson is a central figure among eighteenth-century British Moralists and his extensive treatment of the passions in both ethics and aesthetics helped motivate other influential treatments of them by people such as **Adam Smith** and **David Hume**.

Further reading: Hutcheson 2002

hypothetical imperative: An action is hypothetically imperative if it is what one ought to do on a certain condition, in contrast to being unconditionally or **categorically imperative**. If, for example, you wish to learn to make your own repairs on electrical appliances, you ought to study their workings and get certain sorts of training. But there is no unconditional requirement to learn to repair electrical appliances. In numerous moral theories (and most paradigmatically in **Kant**'s) it is held that moral requirements are categorically and not 'merely' hypothetically imperative. Even supposing that every agent desires **happiness** and that it is rational for each agent to pursue happiness, its pursuit is still hypothetically imperative and not categorically imperative. It is something we ought to do given that we have certain desires. There are theories such

as **Aristotle**'s in which an agent who possesses the **virtues**
recognises certain actions as practically (i.e. morally) necessary. They are actions that a virtuous agent performs
for their own sake and not on account of an independent desire or passion. While this might be interpreted
as a way in which the theory includes the notion of the
categorically imperative, it is still different from Kant's
conception. For Kant, the possession of practical reason
enables any rational agent to grasp what is unconditionally required, what is required independent of desires and
sensibility. For Aristotle, it is only the agent in whom desire and cognition are in agreement – the agent who has
a stable and correct comprehension of what is fine and
just, and wants to act on that basis – who sees virtue's
requirements *as* categorically imperative. A Kantian may
find this a distortion of the notion because it seems to
insert a condition (having a virtuous character and thus
wanting to do what reason requires) that weakens the notion of the categorically imperative beyond recognition.
Whether a moral theory can successfully interpret moral
requirements as hypothetically imperative is a central and
persistent issue. Put the other way round, whether moral
requirements can be interpreted as categorically imperative – as imperative without condition – is a central and
persistent issue in moral theorising.

Further reading: Foot 1978; Kant 1976; Mackie 1990;
McDowell 1978

ideal observer: Some moral theories that are **anti-realist** but
are intended to express the universality and **impartiality**
of moral claims use the notion of an ideal observer to
show how universality and impartiality can be attained.

The view of an informed, unbiased observer takes us to the correct moral judgement even if there are not objects of cognition for moral judgement to converge upon. Some **expressivists** with regard to moral value want to retain distinctive features of moral consideration and moral claims, such as universality and impartiality, and they argue that the ideal observer can succeed at this without concessions to **realism**.

See **impartial spectator, Smith**
Further reading: Firth 1952

immoralism: This is the position that opposes morality and its values, whether or not they are (or are thought to be) objective. The **amoralist** is the person who is unmoved by, or unresponsive to moral considerations. The immoralist has a different stance toward morality, a stance that involves rejection or repudiation.

See **Nietzsche**
Further reading: Nietzsche 1966 and 1998

impartial spectator: In *The Theory of Moral Sentiments* **Adam Smith** developed the notion of the impartial spectator as a way of showing what sorts of considerations and strategies of thought are involved in moral judgement. He referred to the impartial spectator also as '**conscience**' and 'the man within the breast'. The main function of the 'man within the breast' is to attain an **objective** perspective on one's sentiments in order to ascertain what would properly meet with approval from that perspective. Smith grounded moral concern and moral value in the sentiments rather than, for example, *a priori* practical reason as understood by **Kant**, or rational **intuitions** as understood by **Cudworth** or **Clarke**, or **practical wisdom** as understood by **Plato** or **Aristotle**. He also held that there are proper sentiments and thus a basis for correct or incorrect responses and judgements. In that regard the impartial spectator shows how moral judgements based upon affect can nonetheless have the form of cognitive judgements.

Reason is the source of general moral rules, but the origin of our awareness of what is morally right and wrong is in the sentiments. Smith did not think that moral judgements are subjective in the sense that the sentiments one happens to have are sufficient and appropriate as a basis for moral decision and evaluation. While it is pleasant to be approved and praised in one's actions, we recognise the difference between that and being worthy of approval and praise. It is *merit* that can be ascertained by the impartial spectator. Nor is this a roundabout version of **egoism** in which what we ultimately seek is the pleasure of approval by others. Indeed, it is the impartial spectator that enables us to attain clear and correct perceptions of self-love, and that guards against its indulgences and misrepresentations, so that our own self-love can be approved by others. The impartial spectator is not a projection of our stances and dispositions of affect. It enables us to look at our stances, dispositions, decisions and judgements so that we can bring them into agreement with an objective perception of what is merited. To have that capacity is to have a conscience, to be capable of participating in an order governed by morality.

See **ideal observer**

Further reading: Smith 1984

impartiality: This is widely held to be an especially important feature of morality and moral agents. Impartiality requires that judgement concerning what is to be done and concerning what is owed to each person should be independent of considerations about *which* individuals are involved and their particular desires and concerns. Failure to be impartial involves bias, special pleading or other considerations that are distortions of what is morally right or required. There are disputes about whether all of morality must be impartial or whether there are morally appropriate **agent-centred considerations** or types of concern that need not be impartial. For example, acting on the basis of the special concern one has for family members and friends may be interpreted as a morally suspect failure of impartiality, or as a permissible form of partiality (it is not corrupt or invidiously discriminatory), or even as permissible from the impartial point of view. It could be argued that it is impartially proper that one show special kinds of concern for certain people. There may be ways in which certain kinds of concern are defensible from the impartial standpoint. Disputes about the articulation and application of those categories remain central in moral theorising.

See **agent-neutral considerations, Kant, justice**

Further reading: Kant 1976; Nozick 1974; Scheffler 1982

instrumental value: This is value that something has as a means to something else, ultimtely as a means to something valued in its own right or valued as an end. Having painful dental work may be instrumentally valuable for its contribution to health and well-being. The justification of actions or rules of action often depends upon what values are realised, promoted or protected, and it can be crucial to distinguish between what is instrumentally valuable and what is valuable or valued as an end. Typically, moral value is held to be not merely instrumental, though it is not impossible to argue that it is also instrumental in certain respects.

See **intrinsic value**

internalism: In ethics this is the view that the grasp of moral considerations itself has at least some motivational efficacy. The internalist claims that moral considerations and moral motivation are 'internally' connected. **Kant's** moral theory is an example of **rationalist** internalism. He says that to the extent that one grasps moral considerations and takes them to be reasons for acting, rationality alone is sufficient to move us to act. In Kant's view, moral reasons are also motivating considerations. There are also non-cognitivist and **anti-realist** versions of internalism. Such approaches hold that beliefs or any cognitive state cannot account for motivation; cognition or reason is 'practically' inert. Thus, (the argument goes) in order for moral considerations to have any motivational efficacy, they must be non-cognitive. **Hume** developed a view of this kind, as have a host of theorists who find it deeply problematic that moral considerations should both have cognitive content and motivational efficacy. On an **expressivist** view there is an internal relation between one's moral commitments and motivation because the former are themselves grounded in stances, passions or desires; they are just the sorts of states that move us.

A case could be made that **Plato** and **Aristotle** are internalists insofar as **virtue** involves the agreement of reason and desire. In knowing the good – genuinely knowing it – the agent is motivated to realise it in his activity. At least for *that* agent, a correct grasp of moral considerations will move the agent to act. Their views are not 'pure' examples of either rationalist internalism or expressivist internalism.

The debate over internalism and **externalism** cuts across a number of other divides (e.g. **cognitivism/non-cognitivism, consequentialism/non-consequentialism, hedonism**/non-hedonism, and so on) and is focused on the question of what is required for moral motivation.

See **Mill**

Further reading: Hume 1975 and 1978; Kant 1976; Korsgaard 1997; Nagel 1970 and 1986; Williams 1981

intrinsic value: The notion of intrinsic value has been interpreted in at least the following ways. According to the first, something has intrinsic value if it has value in itself and not on account of being *valued* on the basis of any interest or desire. According to the second, something has intrinsic value if its value is unconditioned, not dependent upon anything else being the case, including whatever may be brought about by whatever is intrinsically valuable. In another view, something has intrinsic value if it is desired for its own sake and not for the sake of anything else. It has value as an end in itself, even though it may be conditioned in the respect that it has value because it is desired.

Mill understood pleasure to have value in this way. In his view, pleasure is valued as an end and only as an end; for that reason it is good as an end. However, its being good as an end is dependent upon its being the ultimate object of desire. This notion of intrinsic value is much the same as the notion of something having value as an end and not as a means. **Kant**'s conception of the value of the good will seems to include both of the first two kinds of value. The value of the good will is not in any respect dependent upon its being valued as an object of desire or the satisfaction of an inclination. Nor is its value dependent upon anything else being the case. **Aristotle**'s conception of *eudaimonia* (**happiness** or flourishing) seems to involve the first and third of these conceptions; it has value as an end and only as an end, *and* it is desired for its own sake.

See **axiology, hedonism, Moore**

Further reading: Aristotle 1985; Kant 1976; Mill 1979; Moore 1994; Plato 1992

intuitionism: Two forms of intuitionism are important in ethics. In one form, exemplified by **G. E. Moore**, intuitionism is the view that moral value – good (in Moore's case) – is an object of **cognitive** intuition. That is, we encounter good in a non-inferential cognition, even if we have to develop an understanding of the conditions and circumstances in which good is likely to be present. It is important that Moore did not think that good would just show up anywhere, without dependence upon certain non-moral facts and properties. Good is real, **objective**, and not definable. The other main form of intuitionism in ethics is the view that we have intuitive, non-inferential knowledge of what are our moral duties. **W. D. Ross** held this view. This does not mean that we thoughtlessly know what is morally required. Rather, it is the view that we intuitively know certain *prima facie* moral requirements, for example that a promise is to be fulfilled, or that gratitude is owed to a benefactor, or that reparation is owed to a person we have harmed. In Ross's view '*prima facie*' does not mean 'merely apparent'. *Prima facie* duties are genuine and objective, but in order to know just what is morally required we need to take into account all of the morally relevant features of a situation. Hence, our actual duty depends upon the whole situation. It depends upon the situation, all things considered. There may be a number of morally relevant features such that, for example, in a given case, it would be permissible not to keep a promise, because of another moral consideration having more weight. Moral judgement often requires careful thought, but *prima facie* duties – objects of moral intuition – are a crucial part of what needs to be considered. Moore and Ross had different views of what it is that is known by intuition, but they agreed that as an epistemological matter intuitions are essential to morality.

See **coherentism, foundationalism, non-cognitivism, Prichard**

Further reading: Moore 1994; Prichard 1912; Ross 1930

is/ought distinction: In modern philosophy one of the main issues for ethical theorising has been the relation between factual claims about what is so and normative claims, claims about what ought to be done. In his *Treatise* **Hume** famously remarked that he had seen in the works of several theorists a transition from claims about what there is to claims about what there should be or what should be done, and that he wondered at how this transition could be made without remark or inquiry. He explicitly raised the issue of what could constitute a justification for the transition, or at least its intelligibility. If the transition is a matter of inference, and moral statements can be derived from non-moral statements, this would surely be worthy of note, and we should be able to identify the rule of inference.

Indeed, in the time since Hume drew attention to it, the matter has attracted very considerable remark and inquiry, and many philosophers raise **sceptical** doubts about its justification. To many of them, the inference from 'thus and such are the facts' to 'this is what ought to be done' *because* those are the facts, has seemed suspect and has been the basis for all manner of unsupportable normative claims. **Emotivists** and **prescriptivists** often regard the alleged invalidity of such inferences as one of the grounds for their positions. **Natural law** theories quite explicitly make the case for deriving 'oughts' from what 'is' and they are often criticised for including illicit inferences from 'is' to 'ought' in their conceptions of what are proper human ends. If we cannot validly infer from what is, to what ought to be, the attempt to identify certain ends as right ends for human beings is bound to fail. If we explain that people regard X as good *because* they desire X, or *because* it is a long-standing custom to pursue X, and the like, it only shows why people think they ought to do certain things. That is an unproblematic empirical project, and it does not show that there are 'oughts' built into the world, or into the facts. There are empirical 'becauses' and there are logical 'becauses' but there is no basis for 'oughts' that have any standing apart from desires, interests, stances, commitments or choices. One of the main reasons offered for scepticism in regard to the is/ought relation concerns the issue of how any fact or state of affairs or any belief about it could have action-guiding efficacy.

Moral considerations are (it is generally agreed) action-guiding; they have prescriptive significance. How, it is asked, could the grasp of any factual consideration be action-guiding or prescriptive in its own right? For pre-scriptivity to enter the picture some choice or attitude or stance is needed. Suppose I believe that I ought to assist a person in distress because I desire to see them out of difficulty, or because my upbringing shaped a habit of willingness to help and a tendency to feel blameworthy for not doing what I can to help. In each of those cases it is the desire or the habit of affect that explains why I think I ought to help and how I am motivated to help. The fact that the person is in distress is just that; it's a fact, not a fact that also has a normative dimension or significance. It *seems* to have those, but that is because of dispositions of affect or inclination. We might argue that that is the kind of sensibility people ought to have, but that does not alter the main issue. It simply bumps it to a different level – the level of what is desirable in people in general.

Hume did not actually say that the transition could not be made. He did say that he had never *seen* it made. In the time since he remarked on it many philosophers have argued that it could not be made. That view is common to all versions of **expressivism**, moral **anti-realism**, and **non-cognitivism**. In early articulations of **emotivism** (e.g. by A. J. **Ayer**) the argument is explicit and carries a lot of the weight in making the case for emotivism. Being neither empirical claims subject to standard tests of confirmation, nor logical or analytic claims, normative claims fail to report or express **objective** normative significance. There just is no such thing.

In **J. L. Mackie**'s formulation of the issue, if there were objective 'oughts' that would be tantamount to there being categorical imperatives built into the structure of reality – features of reality disclosing what ought to be done independent of being conditional upon anyone's desires, attitudes, concerns and choices. Mackie argued that the problem is not that this violates a criterion of cognitive meaningfulness. The problem is that we have no reason to believe this is true. In particular, realism about 'oughts' would involve attributing action-guiding efficacy to facts, something he regarded as utterly mysterious. Mackie even offered several hypotheses about *why* people believe there are objective values or categorical imperatives.

Defenders of objective values, both naturalists and non-naturalists have replied to the sceptical challenges with a number of different arguments. Some have a basically **Aristotelian** pedigree and develop the claim that there are perfectly intelligible ways in which we can recognise how reason and desire – or cognition and sensibility – can be in agreement, insofar as desire aims at what reason understands to be good. There is nothing exotic or unintelligible about the notion of *correct* desire, given what it is to be a rational animal, a being with a human nature. Indeed, it is *prima facie* implausible that there should not be objective goods and excellences of character for creatures constituted as we are. Other approaches involve arguing that moral facts and properties can be explicated as being constituted by, or even identical with non-moral facts and properties, without being logically or analytically derivable from them. It is also possible to argue that moral considerations do not necessarily have motivational efficacy. If that is the case, the argument that the prescriptivity of moral facts is a mystery is deflected to some extent, though it leaves open the issue of just how objective moral considerations are related to motives.

See **Open Question Argument**

Further reading: Foot 1978 and 2001; Frankena 1939; Hare 1973; Hume 1975 and 1978; Mackie 1990; Moore 1994

justice: Justice is a crucial concern with regard to laws, institutional arrangements, actions and practices. A paradigmatic example of its importance is **Plato**'s treatment of it, which involved theorising about the soul, the organisation and rule of the state, and fundamental questions about what is good for its own sake and what makes a life a good life in contrast to simply being one that happens to be enjoyed. Justice concerns some of the most basic **rights** and obligations and, in general, is a central issue in the relations between persons in both the moral and political contexts. While the diversity of accounts of justice is quite considerable, two of the main concerns of justice are (a) the distribution of benefits and burdens in a society, and (b) why and how wrongdoers are to be punished. The former is the issue of distributive justice and the latter is the issue of **retributive** justice.

Distributive justice has been explicated in a large number of ways, including accounts in terms of merit, contribution, equality, **utility** and mutual benefit among other possibilities. There are conceptual issues (What is the relevant kind of consideration in seeing to it that each person is served justly?), empirical issues (How is that just distribution to be achieved?), and normative issues (Why is that the relevant notion of what is due to each?). Theorising about retributive justice has exhibited the same complexity. Views in that context include accounts in terms of desert, utility, correction, denunciation and annulment of a crime by a proportional infliction of harm or deprivation. In addition, many moral philosophers have theorised about the grounds or basis for justice, and whether it is grounded in **natural law** and **natural rights**, or in the usefulness of certain general rules and expectations, or certain conventions that people agree upon, or *a priori* considerations, or perhaps some other basis. Justice has been traditionally regarded as one of the main **virtues** of a moral agent and there is an extensive literature on why that should be so, and on the relation of justice to other virtues, and what would motivate an agent to have a concern for justice. Moreover, it is widely held that there is a crucial relation between justice and **impartiality**, and that the just agent is impartial in judgement.

See **Grotius, Hobbes, punishment**

Further reading: Aristotle 1985; Grotius 2004; Hobbes 1991; Kant 1976; Locke 1988; Nietzsche 1998; Plato 1992; Rawls 1971

Kant, Immanuel (1724–1804) German: Kant's ethical theory is widely regarded as a paradigmatic version of **deontology**. Kant argued that moral requirements are distinctive in that they are **categorically imperative,** that is they are unconditional requirements, not dependent upon any particular desires or passions. In Kant's view there is a fundamental connection between rationality, **autonomy** and morality. Persons (rational agents) are capable of acting on the basis of principles that could be **impartially** endorsed by all other persons. That is, persons can act on the basis of what is rationally required regardless of their inclinations and feelings. Those unconditioned rational principles – principles that meet that criterion of **universalisability** – are moral principles. They are **objective** in the sense that they are universal and necessary, rather than being objective by representing value-entities. In acting on such principles persons exercise autonomy, the ability to act on a law of their own making and to answer to the authority of their own reason. This self-legislation is what is distinctive of rational agency in contrast to any other kind of causality (e.g. **naturalistic** causality). The exercise of that agency is the locus of moral value. Value that is conditioned in any manner is value that is dependent on causes other than rational agency and could be brought about by means other than rational volition. That would still be genuine value but not *moral* value because morality concerns the nature of rational volition. 'Am I doing the right thing because it is the right thing to do?' is the question the answer to which reveals moral worth (or its absence).

The distinction between obligation and inclination is crucial to Kant's ethics. He argues that in our awareness of ourselves as agents we can recognise those different sources of motivation and reasons for action. Examination of the concept of moral obligation brings its unconditioned character into relief, setting it apart from all other grounds for action. Morally worthy actions not only accord with what the moral law requires but are also done out of respect for that law. The notion that reason can be practical – that reason on its own can supply both a conception of what is to be done and a sufficient motive for acting – is at the core of Kant's moral theorising. He held that there are laws of reason that are distinct from laws of nature, and in being grounded solely in reason they can be ascertained *a priori*. The moral law is one of them. Thus, in moral thought and action, the principles we think with have their ground in pure practical reason, reason that is action-guiding independent of any empirical desires, passions, interests and dispositions.

In that respect, Kant's is an **internalist** theory, one in which moral considerations have motivational efficacy at least to the extent that we respond rationally to them. Kant was anxious to show that the sciences, which were increasingly showing the natural world to be a unified system operating in accord with deterministic laws, did not threaten the genuineness of morality. Unlike events in nature, reason operates according to laws of its own making. Rational beings can be responsive to normative considerations – considerations about what they *ought* to do – and in Kant's account of this the general form of the categorical imperative is presented as the criterion for ascertaining moral duties. He regarded the criterion of universalisability as equivalent to a test in terms of always respecting persons as ends in themselves and never treating them merely as means. Persons are owed **respect** because of their rational **autonomy**, their capacity for self-legislation. For that reason they are never to be regarded or treated merely as instruments or objects of the purposes of others.

Despite the philosophical complexity and difficulty of Kant's theory he meant to show that the theoretically untutored moral awareness of the ordinary person is a reliable moral guide and judge. This is because just by virtue of being rational each of us is able to recognise the crucial distinctions between obligation and inclination, duty and desire, and treating persons and ends merely as means. In addition, his theory has been influential in a great deal of subsequent ethical theorising, especially in theorising in which the distinctive status of persons as free and equal participants in the moral order is a key notion. In recent years a number of thinkers have appealed to Kantian considerations concerning the form and rational basis of moral principles even if they do not also accept his metaphysical account of rational agency.

See **externalism, intrinsic value**

Further reading: Donagan 1977; Kant 1965, 1976 and 1980; Rawls 1997

Kierkegaard, Soren (1813–55) Danish: Now recognised as a seminal thinker with regard to **existentialism**, Kierkegaard was a strong critic of **Hegel**'s idealism and sought to restore individual, subjective, existential concern and focus to the centre of thinking about life and values. His thought has had considerable influence in twentieth-century Protestant theology, and Kierkegaard himself took theological questions to be fundamental. He characterised different fundamental ways of life – the aesthetic, the ethical, and the religious – and he explicated them and the relations between them in terms of choice. In this way he explored the individual's confrontation with his own freedom and the necessity to choose; to make a choice without being guided by authoritative criteria. That indeed, is the nature of radical choice. Through the radical choice that one makes in being a Christian the individual comes into contact with the **objective** reality of God through faith (because Christianity involves paradoxes inscrutable to reason). In that sense, the choice that one makes to climb out of the dread experienced in confronting one's own freedom is radically **subjective** but makes possible an encounter with an objective reality.

See **Nietzsche, Sartre, voluntarism**

Further reading: Kierkegaard 1971, 1972, 1973 and 1974

Locke, John (1632–1704) English: Locke argued that a demonstrative moral science was possible but he did not develop that science. His importance in ethics is based mainly on his theory of **natural law** and social **contract**. In the *Second Treatise of Government* Locke elaborated an account of the **state of nature, natural rights,** natural law, and the establishment of legitimate political authority on the basis of a social contract. In that respect, his account of natural rights and obligations, accessible to any rational agent, indicates at least some of how he might have conceptualised ethics. Locke believed that there are laws of reason that can guide the establishment of political authority and institutions, and that there are normative measures for whether rulers and their policies are legitimate. Rational individuals are willing to give up some of their natural liberty to enforce the law of nature, in order to make the conditions of life more orderly and less precarious, by establishment of public authority and the promulgation of laws formulated by representatives of those who are to obey that authority. He argued that legitimate authority required the consent of the governed and it must protect and respect each individual's person and property. His notion of property extended to the point regarding the individual as having possession of his own person. The focus on the individual was not a basis for

acquisitive **egoism,** but for defining a protected sphere
around each person, securing certain basic kinds of inviolability. Locke's account of the right to property, and
its importance to the individual and to self-determination
have been crucial to the development of classical liberal
political theory.

See **Grotius, Hobbes**

Further reading: Grotius 2004; Hobbes 1991; Locke
1988

love: In some moral theorising love has a central role in relation to the good. For example, in some of **Plato**'s works,
love is what makes the Forms objects toward which we
strive; it is the desire to recover the knowledge and truth
that are blocked for us by the distractions and exigen-
cies of life in the natural world. For **Aristotle,** the virtuous agent loves what is just and noble, and takes delight
in virtuous activity and in the **virtue** of other excellent
agents. In his view the best kind of friendship is a part-
nership in virtue in which each party seeks the good of
the other for the sake of the other. In these conceptions
and in Jewish and Christian conceptions, the good has
an attractive power, and love is that through which we
seek to attain or realise or come in contact with the good
(or with God, in the religious traditions). Love, or rather
loving what merits love, is a way for us to realise fully,
complete, or perfect our nature. In the religious tradition it is through loving God that we are perfected, and
God's grace, which is necessary to make that possible,
is a kind of love for us (though God does not need to
be completed or perfected). In secular theorising love often takes the form of a generalised **benevolence,** a genuine and felt sympathetic concern for the good of others that is more than just good will and more than just
affection.

Sympathy (broadly understood) and **benevolence** were prominent features of much of British moral theorising in the eighteenth century, in part perhaps as a response to conceptions of human nature and moral motivation that made self-interest so central – conceptions found in thinkers such as **Hobbes** and **Mandeville**.

See **perfectionism, teleology**

Further reading: Aquinas 1998; Aristotle 1985; Augustine 1998; Hobbes 1991; Maimonides 1956 and 1975; Mandeville 1924; Plato 1992

McDowell, John (1942–) English: In recent metaethical debates McDowell has articulated and defended a version of **virtue-centred** moral **realism** that develops resources from **Aristotle**'s moral psychology and the later Wittgenstein's philosophy of mind and language. This is meant to provide an account of moral reasoning, discourse and judgement that is a realist account without problematic ontological commitments, and that shows the centrality of the **virtues** to moral thought and action. The approach borrows from Aristotle with regard to the complementary roles of cognition and sensibility, and it borrows from Wittgenstein with regard to the conception of judgement being rule-governed but not in a codifiable manner. McDowell has progressively developed and revised his view (attributing increasing importance to the Aristotelian notion of a second nature) in a number of articles and books over the last twenty-five years.

See **metaethics**

Further reading: McDowell 1978, 1979, 1988 and 1997

MacIntyre, Alasdair (1929–) American: MacIntyre has been instrumental in motivating a reconsideration of **virtue-centred** ethics and theories of practical rationality. He has developed his view through a critique of Enlightenment and post-Enlightenment morality, which he finds to be strained by some fundamental incoherencies and lacking a sound and tenable basis in moral anthropology. These defects undermine the liberal individualism so ambitiously shaped by Enlightenment thinking. His work has moved steadily in the direction of a more Aristotelian and Thomistic character combined with an emphasis on the significance of tradition in moral epistemology, moral education, and the relation between **virtues** and principles in the overall conception of practical rationality.

See **Aquinas, Aristotle**

Further reading: MacIntyre 1981 and 1988

Mackie, John L. (1917–82) Australian: Mackie wrote widely in philosophy. His most important work in ethics was *Ethics: Inventing Right and Wrong*. He argued that there are no **objective** values even though, in his view, in making moral judgements people typically assume that there are objective values. Mackie sought to explicate why and how this is so, and he also provided an account of the status of moral value along **subjectivist** lines. A crucial element of his view is that he does not reject moral objectivity on the grounds that moral discourse has (merely) **non-cognitive** meaning. His view is that in making moral judgements people purport to be making objective claims – but they are mistaken. Moral judgements ordinarily have **cognitive** meaning but they are all false. He called this approach an 'error theory' in order to contrast with approaches based upon linguistic analysis. The main reasons for Mackie's denial of moral objectivity are that objective moral values would have to have a status and nature unlike anything that we (plausibly and correctly) regard as objective, and that correspondingly we would need a special cognitive faculty to detect or perceive objective values. Another key reason is that Mackie thought it mysterious how **prescriptivity** or the **categorically imperative** character often attributed to moral values could be an objective feature or constituent of the world. Mackie's work has been widely discussed in recent **metaethics**.

See **emotivism, expressivism, Hume, intuitionism, naturalism, supervenience**

Further reading: Mackie 1990

Maimonides, Moses (1135–1204) Spanish: A rabbi, theologian, and philosopher, Maimonides sought to integrate Jewish religion and key elements of **Aristotelian** philosophy and science. His works were influential in his time, and have remained key resources of Jewish theology and philosophy. He is a key figure in that current of Jewish thought that is concerned with staying in the rabbinic tradition of interpretation of Judaism, while connecting it to more **rationalistic** and **naturalistic** commitments and explanations. He developed an intellectualist conception of human **perfection**; its most complete realisation in a knowing **love** of God. He also used the Aristotelian **virtue-centred** idiom of **virtue** to explicate Jewish ethics and moral psychology, though his religious commitments involved him in significant departures from Aristotle (for example, concerning specific states of character such as pride and anger). While codifications and commentaries on Jewish law were important only within the Jewish community, his philosophical influence was acknowledged by **Aquinas**, and later on is evident in the works of **Spinoza**.

See **teleology**

Further reading: Maimonides 1956 and 1975; Spinoza 1994

Mandeville, Bernard (c. 1670–1733) Dutch (lived much of his life in England): Mandeville argued that what moralists regard as **vices** – such things as envy, fashion-consciousness, conspicuous consumption, and indulgence – actually promote economic growth and national greatness. Those vices are fuel for the engine of growth and trade and they also lead to the creation of employment for large numbers of people who might otherwise be underemployed or unemployed. If people were concerned only with the production and provision of necessities, there would be far less economic activity and movement and growth of wealth. A society does well by responding to human nature's delight in flattery; it is love of flattery that motivates people to pursue the public interest and not merely their own. Mandeville wrote at an important time in the development of early modern moral theorising and many figures in the British tradition in particular, felt it necessary to respond to him.

See **virtue**

Further reading: Mandeville 1924

metaethics: Metaethical thought concerns the ontology, epistemology and semantics of moral value and moral discourse. The debates in metaethics are not directly about first-order moral issues (e.g. whether capital punishment is justified, whether it is ever permissible to make a deceitful promise, and so on). Metaethics is a second-order project concerning the status and nature of first-order claims as cognitive or non-cognitive, **objective** or **subjective**, *a priori* or empirical, **universal** or **relative**, and so forth. Metaethics also reaches into questions concerning moral motivation. For instance, the issue of whether reason alone is sufficient as a moral motivation or whether there must be some motivational ground in desire or affect is a metaethical matter. The question of whether moral values are properly interpreted

naturalistically is a metaethical issue. The debate concerning whether good is definable – and what sort of definition is at issue – is a metaethical debate. An important and persistent issue is whether metaethics makes a difference to normative ethics. Does one's second-order account of morality only permit or support certain first-order moral claims? For example, a defender of moral **cognitivism** may argue that **non-cognitivism** subverts the authority of moral considerations. The non-cognitivist might argue that morality is not threatened by metaethics, and the course of normative debates is an issue 'inside' first-order morality. Metaethics was given a powerful impetus by **G. E. Moore**'s *Principia Ethica* (first published in 1903). His critique of ethical **naturalism** became a focus for both **realists** and **anti-realists**, and for several decades metaethical concerns dominated English-language moral theorising.

See **emotivism, expressivism, Mackie, prescriptivism, projectivism, supervenience**

Further reading: Ayer 1952; Blackburn 1993 and 1998; Brink 1989; McDowell 1979, 1988 and 1997; Mackie 1990; Moore 1994

Mill, John Stuart (1806–73) English: A key figure in the development of **utilitarian** moral theory, and author of *Utilitarianism*. He defended consequentialist **hedonism**. This was part of his attempt to put moral theory on an **objective**, empirical basis. He argued that pleasure and pleasure alone is desired for its own sake, and thus good. Accordingly, actions are to be evaluated on the basis of how much pleasure overall they bring about. Mill departed from his predecessor **Bentham** in making a case for qualitative distinctions among pleasures. Mill thought that even with such distinctions, it was still possible to succeed at objective, empirical measurement of utility. He argued that the preferences of those people who have the widest breadth of experience could be used as the criteria for which pleasures are inferior and which are superior. He felt that utilitarianism needed to accommodate the ranking of pleasures on more than just quantitative grounds in order to avoid the charge of being a vulgar hedonism, of being a theory of value with a base or ignoble conception of what humans can be and strive for. With the same concern in mind, he also argued that **virtue** can be desired for its own sake as part of **happiness,** even though an agent's concern for virtue must first be motivated by finding virtuous activity pleasing. In this way, Mill sought to make a case for excellences of character and informed, correct judgement concerning pleasure, while remaining faithful to a hedonist theory of value and a consequentialist moral theory. Mill also saw the need to show how **justice** could be explicated on utilitarian grounds. He has been enormously influential both with regard to issues concerning the main structure of moral theory (e.g. **consequentialism**) and with regard to his theory of value (hedonism that acknowledges qualitative distinctions between pleasures).

Mill's *On Liberty* focuses on politics rather than moral theory but there is an important connection between them. His political theorising makes a case for a high degree of individual freedom, and that freedom is important to individuals' fashioning and pursuing their conceptions of a good life. In that regard, there may be a crucial link between political **autonomy** and the promotion of utility in Mill's thought.

See **cognitivism, naturalism**

Further reading: Bentham 1996; Mill 1979; Smart and Williams 1973

monism: Value monism is the view that there is one fundamental value or source or ground of moral value. For example, to argue that **utility** alone has moral value is to argue for a version of monism. And to argue that pleasure alone is the source of value is a type of monism. Similarly, to argue that the good **will** has unique and sole moral value is to argue for a version of monism. A monistic theory may include many different principles and moral rules, but there is just one basic value or source of value.

See **pluralism**

Further reading: Nagel 1985; Raz 1986

Moore, G. E. (1873–1958) English: Moore's *Principia Ethica* set the agenda for a great deal of the metaethical theorising since its first publication in 1903. Moore was an **intuitionist,** holding that good is real, **objective,** and an object of **cognition.** He argued that **naturalistic** approaches are bound to fail because exhaustively explicating or analysing good in terms of any other properties, facts or entities would actually be a way of showing that it is not a distinct reality – it is, we might say, 'nothing but' something else. For example, if it is ture that good can be defined as 'what maximises happiness for the greatest number of people', then good is not a distinct entity or property in its own right. But, Moore insisted, when we encounter good we have before our minds something distinct from whatever analysis or definition of it that may be offered. His **'Open Question Argument'** was intended to show this. Define good however one likes, we can still ask of anything that satisfies that definition, 'Is it good?' and the question is quite genuine. Suppose an action maximises happiness for the greatest number. Asking if it is also a good action is not trivial or based on a misunderstanding. It is a significant question the answer to which depends upon the presence or absence of good in the overall state of affairs.

Moore argued that any attempt fully to analyse or define good will commit what he called the 'naturalistic fallacy' It may be that what is referred to in the definition is a good thing (e.g. pleasure, what we desire to desire, knowledge, and so on) but it is not just what good is. That latter is simple and undefinable. Good does not occur in the world randomly. Moore held that the presence of good depends upon the presence of other properties and entities. (It **supervenes** on non-moral properties and facts.) Still, that does not (and cannot) show that good is definable in other terms. Moore intended his account of the naturalistic fallacy to apply to any attempts at definition or analysis of good, including those that involve non-empirical and metaphysical elements.

His influence has been profound. Some **realists** and especially **non-naturalists** rely upon his arguments to make the case for moral value being objective. He provides a basis for interpreting moral value in other than **projectivist** or **expressivist** terms. **Anti-realists** see in his work the resources to show that naturalism cannot succeed. Even though anti-realists understand moral value in ways that are very remote from Moore's account, they credit him with developing powerful critical tools with which naturalism and metaphysical and theological ethics can be dismantled.

See **Mackie, Ross**

Further reading: Ayer 1952; Brink 1989; Blackburn 1993 and 1998; Frankena 1939; Hare 1973; Mackie 1990; Moore 1994; Prichard 1992; Ross 1930

moral luck: See **fortune.**

moral sense: Moral sense theories are accounts of moral judgement and moral motivation intended to avoid what seemed to be **rationalist** excesses on the one hand, and subjectivist and egoist excesses on the other. Shaftesbury and **Hutcheson** are key figures in the development of moral sense theorising. They held that our perceptions of actions or states of character (using 'perception' quite broadly) elicit feelings or affective responses that are indicative of the moral **virtue** or **vice** of what is perceived. In this way, sensibility has a key role in moral judgement though the moral properties that are sensed are not themselves subjective. Moral sense enables us to be aware of moral properties and because moral sense is a mode of affect it also influences motivation. The moral sense theorists put moral theorising on a path that was later refined and elaborated by thinkers such as **Hume** and **Smith**.

See **Clarke, Cudworth, impartial spectator**

Further reading: Hume 1975 and 1978; Hutcheson 2002; Smith 1984

Murdoch, Iris (1919–99) English: Both a novelist and a philosopher, Murdoch has had an important role in reigniting interest in moral **realism** through her critique of **expressivism** and **voluntarism**. She did not develop a moral theory or a systematic articulation of moral realism but her treatments of the nature and the objects of moral concern have leant themselves to reinforcing realist conceptions of value. In particular, her critique of all forms of expressivism and voluntarism opened paths for realist accounts of value and moral thought. Her work exhibits a deep intertwining of moral anthropology and the epistemology and ontology of value. Murdoch paid close attention to moral phenomenology as part of an effort to stay close to actual moral experience and the features of moral life. Her novels also reflect these concerns and approaches.

Further reading: Murdoch 1985

N

natural law: Numerous approaches plausibly fall under the heading 'natural law' but two have been especially prominent. In one view, ethics is based upon natural law in the sense that there are principles of well-ordered activity, the kind that realises human good. Those principles have their ground in human nature and can be ascertained by reflection upon it. Many theorists of this type of natural law have also included theological elements in their view, holding that natural law has its ground in the natures of things given through God's creation and providence. However, the approach is not necessarily committed to any theological claims. One could develop a **teleological** natural law account that is **naturalistic**. A natural law theory does not have to involve commitment to the existence of any **non-natural** beings or agency. Still, the best-known natural law theorising of this first type is probably **Aquinas**'s and variants of it in the Catholic tradition. This first type is teleological in the respect that the laws of nature in question are essentially normative considerations for human activity, given a conception of perfected (fully actualised) human nature. That is, given the capacities constitutive of human nature, there are fundamental normative principles of well-ordered human life, and these are the basis for ethical theory. The proper operation of those capacities actualises human good. Knowledge of natural law is the basis for **practical wisdom**, and it enables agents to deliberate and act well – to acquire and exercise the virtues. Natural law approaches of this kind are rivals to ethical theories grounded in **subjectivity**, sentiment or decision. A natural law theory holds that there are basic ethical considerations independent of convention or decision and that they are universal and can be comprehended by reason.

A second type of natural law theory focuses more on what a rational agent would recognise or agree to as necessary to leading a life such that an agent regards as worthwhile and desirable. The role of agreement or endorsement by rational agents does not make the approach a subjectivist strategy. Rather, these views are strategies of ascertaining basic requirements on a moral theory by tests structured to meet conditions of rational acceptance. **Hobbes**'s and **Locke**'s theories of the state of nature and the social **contract** are theories of this type. So is **Rawls**'s theory of **justice**. Those approaches are not shaped by a teleological conception of human nature and human good. Instead, they conceptualise human agency apart from the particular circumstances of any specific individuals' lives, and ascertain the principles and arrangements that are acceptable to anyone, just considered as a rational agent. There is a role for construction of principles in this approach that is not found in the other approach, but the construction is guided by what are held to be rational requirements, rather than considerations that could be interpreted as indicating **relativism**. Thus, some variants of natural law theorising involve a social contract, while others (e.g. Aquinas's) do not.

In both approaches the theorist's philosophical anthropology is crucial. That is what, upon analysis, leads to the theory's results. The conception of human nature or of rational agency upon which the theorising is based will point the theory or the social contract it validates in certain directions. Whether the theorist uses the methodological strategy of positing a **state of nature** or an **original position**, the liberties and interests of individuals in the one or the other will be crucial to the justification of the theory's substantive conclusions.

Among the sources of natural law theorising, the **Stoics** and **Aristotle** are important. The Stoics understood ethics in the context of an overall theory of the world and the natures of things, such that an excellent human life is a life of virtue through which the individual lives according to nature. Our reason enables us to discern genuine value and the way to lead life accordingly. Aristotle's conception of an end proper to human nature and the role of practical wisdom in realising it were also important influences.

See **perfectionism**

Further reading: Aquinas 1998; Aristotle 1985; Grotius 2004; Hobbes 1991; Locke 1988; Rawls 1971; Veatch 2003

natural rights: A natural right is a right that is not conferred upon a person and cannot be withdrawn or taken away though, of course, it can be violated. A theory of natural rights has to provide an account of their ground and an account of why certain specific rights have this fundamental status. How do we ascertain which rights are natural? What is it about certain rights and not others, which defines them as natural rights? Early modern theorists such as **Hobbes, Locke** and **Grotius** are key figures in theorising on this matter. They held that prior to the establishment of legitimate political authority individuals have certain rights just as rational agents with concern for their security and property. For example, even in the **state of nature** an agent has the right of **retribution**; the right to punish another for being harmed. There may be some natural rights one should be willing to surrender in entering into a social **contract**; Hobbes certainly held this view. The civil condition provides institutions and procedures for just administration that are lacking in the state of nature. Whether a theorist holds that natural rights are fully carried into the civil state or that some are rationally surrendered in it, the conception of natural rights is central to a great deal of modern thought concerning the ground and permissible character and scope of political authority.

See **original position**

Further reading: Grotius 2000; Hobbes 1991; Locke 1988; Rousseau 1946

naturalism: There are naturalist positions in several different areas of philosophy and there are several different interpretations of naturalism. In the context of ethics, a naturalist position is one that holds that moral value can be explicated or interpreted without reference to anything other than the kinds of entities and properties that are accessible to observation and the natural and social sciences. In this view values do not have a metaphysical status separate from natural objects and their features. **Mill's** **utilitarianism** is an example of ethical naturalism. According to that view, moral value is understood in terms of pleasure, that which is desired for its own sake and only for its own sake. Pleasure is an empirically accessible, natural, psychological phenomenon. We are to promote utility, with utility understood in terms of pleasure. **Hume's** moral theory is another example of ethical naturalism. He explains moral judgement in terms of feeling, rejecting the view that values are **objective** features of things knowable by reason or by sense perception or a special **moral sense**. Moral value and moral judgement are to be explicated in terms of sentiments, passions, responses, concerns – phenomena that are matters of feeling rather than knowledge. Factual beliefs are still important, in that often we have the sentiments that we have because of what the facts are. But a moral evaluation does not refer to a moral fact. This is different from Mill's approach, in which the question of how much utility an action or a practice has is an objective, factual matter (at least comparatively).

Some thinkers regard **Aristotle**'s ethical theory as naturalistic, on account of the centrality of his notion of a real, intrinsic end proper to human nature, and the way in which that end is realised through virtuous activity. While there are disputes about just how naturalism should be interpreted, there are also clear examples of thinkers whose conceptions of moral value are **non-naturalistic**, for instance, **Plato, Hare** and **Kant**.

See **cognitivism, metaethics, realism, supervenience**
Further reading: Aristotle 1985; Brink 1989; Hare 1963 and 1973; Mill 1979; Moore 1994

Nietzsche, Friedrich (1844–1900) German: His philosophy has been the subject of very animated interpretive disputes, and thinkers with very diverse views claim his influence. Nietzsche developed a powerful critique of the sort of moral **rationalism** of **Kantian** theorising and he argued that human beings are value-creators in an activity of self-affirmation. Via rich and vivid aphorism and metaphor he argued that in order properly to understand value we must explore its genealogy. One thing it will show is that the ways in which, and the reasons for which values, ideals and practices originally came to be might be quite different from the rationales we supply for them. In that respect, Nietzsche can be seen as including a **naturalistic** aspect to his treatment of morality, along with something of an **existentialist** dimension on account of the weight put on choice, value creation, and responsibility for it. A crucial feature of his view of morality is that morals as widely understood reflect a powerful project of repression of human drives. Moreover, this repression often issues in resentment and it, in turn, powerfully shapes values.

In the history of morality one of the key results of that repression is 'slave' morality, a morality in which equality, compassion, **altruism**, guilt and humility are central. This is actually a way for the weaker, the more diffident, and the more resentful to restrain those stronger and bolder in spirit. Ultimately, value creation (including when it is not self-conscious and deliberate) is an exercise of 'the will to power', which is a basic drive that can be directed at others or can be directed inwardly, as in slave morality.

Nietzsche's thought developed and changed over time, but it is fair to say that overall he investigated morality as a phenomenon with a history, the exploration of which is crucial to understanding human values. That history reveals ways in which people have thought they were in possession of rational justifications when in fact they were not. Scrutiny of that history and identification of the drives that motivate and direct the creation of values show that what has passed for objective values and fundamental moral requirements is really something quite other. Nietzsche also used the results of his examination of morality as the basis for proposing a new vision of value creation in which the free expression of the will to power, unshackled by repression and rationalisation, affirms human freedom in a way that morality had made impossible. He sees his project as an examination of the value of morality itself.

Further reading: Nietzsche 1966 and 1998

nihilism: This is the view that moral judgements cannot be justified, or that there are no moral values. There are other positions that are sometimes regarded as versions of nihilism by their opponents; for example, defenders of the view that God is the source of moral values might regard atheists as nihilists. There is nothing necessarily nihilistic about atheism, but the theist might regard the view that we create or choose values as a kind of nihilism, because it seems to ground values in arbitrariness.

Nietzsche can be regarded as a nihilist and the term was part of his idiom for discussing morality. However, while he was a powerful critic of traditional (theistic or **rationalistic**) morality, he did not claim that there are no values at all or that values simply reflect preferences or arbitrary feelings. 'Nihilism' tends to have a negative (even menacing) connotation, and it is often used in a condemnatory manner. It is important to attend to just what claims and commitments are being called 'nihilist' in order to see whether the nihilist is rejecting morality altogether (and in what sense) or propounding a conception that is indeed a conception of value, but not one that meets the conditions of the critic.

See **amoralism, existentialism, immoralism**

Further reading: Kierkegaard 1971, 1972, 1973 and 1974; Nietzsche 1966 and 1998; Sartre 1947

non-cognitivism: In ethics this is the view that moral claims and judgements express or reflect attitudes, choices or stances, and that they do not report moral facts. The non-cognitivist denies what the **cognitivist** asserts, namely that moral considerations are objective and that moral judgements can be evaluated as being objectively true or false. Moral non-cognitivists need not assert that morality is somehow less genuine or important than we take it to be. Some non-cognitivists are interested in explaining how moral claims have full-fledged significance even though there are no moral facts. **Hume** is perhaps an example of that approach. Contemporary expressivists such as **Blackburn** are Hume-influenced non-cognitivists. Other non-cognitivists argue that because non-cognitivism is a correct account of morality, moral claims have only emotive meaning and *therefore*, there is no such thing as being morally correct or morally mistaken, even if we believe strongly that some things are right and others wrong.

See **Ayer, emotivism, intuitionism, metaethics, projectivism**

Further reading: Ayer 1952; Blackburn 1993 and 1998; Hare 1963 and 1973; Hume 1975 and 1978

non-consequentialism: Any theory that does not locate moral value entirely in the states of affairs that actions bring about is a non-consequentialist theory. Among the most influential non-consequentialist theories are **deontological** approaches that regard certain action-types as intrinsically right or wrong, and make moral rights and duties central. Another type of non-consequentialism is **virtue-centred theory** in which the moral value of actions depends, at least in part, upon the dispositions and judgement of the agent. In virtue-centred approaches the agent's character, as reflected in action, is crucial to the moral quality of action. **Kant**'s moral theory, and **Aristotle**'s, are examples of non-consequentialist approaches. A theory need not be a 'pure' **consequentialism** or 'pure' non-consequentialism. However, to the extent that different kinds of considerations properly figure in moral evaluation and deliberation, their relations and weights need to be explicated as fully as possible so that it is clear when and why certain considerations (e.g. an **absolute** prohibition) apply even though other considerations point in a different direction.

See **Bentham, Mill**

Further reading: Anscombe 1958; Aristotle 1985; Kant 1976; Ross 1930; Scheffler 1982

non-naturalism: This is the view that moral value cannot be explicated or interpreted in terms of **naturalistic** facts or properties. Moral values have a status and nature distinct from facts and properties accessible to sense perception and the empirical sciences. **Plato**'s Form of the Good is a paradigmatic example of non-naturalism, as is **Kant's** conception of the good will. **Moore's** arguments to show that good cannot be defined, and that it is not *nothing but* something else (e.g. what is desired for its own sake, what we desire to desire, what is most pleasing, and so on) are meant to show that good is real, **objective**, and non-natural.

The non-naturalist need not argue that moral value has *no* relation to naturalistic phenomena. Still, moral value is understood as really distinct from naturalistic entities or properties, even when the presence of value depends upon their presence. For example, an arrangement in which each person's holdings are in accord with fairness – each has what she deserves, given her legitimate claims – is a morally good arrangement. The goodness *depends* upon the distribution, but cannot be exhaustively defined or interpreted in terms of it. It is a good situation, but that situation is not exactly the same thing as *good*; that is the point of recognising and judging it to be a situation with the property *good*. The value has a reality of its own. Some non-naturalists argue that we have a capacity for moral **intuition**, a cognitive capacity to detect moral properties. In this context 'intuition' refers to non-inferential cognitive awareness. (It is not a hunch or a feeling.)

One key concern of non-naturalists is that if moral value could be explicated naturalistically, it would be explained away. There would not be anything it is in its own right. The intuitionist argues that to explicate exhaustively moral properties in terms of anything non-moral would not show moral value to be naturalistic; it would show that there is no such thing as moral value. There are non-naturalists who are not intuitionists. Kant held that only the good will was unconditionally good and that the law of volition for a good will is a law of pure practical reason. The moral law can be ascertained *a priori*. This is a different philosophical project from showing that moral value is an object of intuition. For the intuitionist moral properties are objective features or constituents of the world and they are accessible to us by a cognitive act of recognising and comprehending them. For Kant, the moral law is **objective**, but that is because it reflects a universal, necessary, unconditioned principle of volition, and not a feature of the world.

Many moral naturalists hold that moral judgements are indeed cognitive judgements and that they are true or false by virtue of the moral facts. They might argue that moral facts are constituted by non-moral facts, or that moral facts **supervene** on non-moral facts, without the former requiring a faculty of intuition in order to be detected. Part of what makes the issue complicated is that naturalism can take a number of different forms. The form that Moore was anxious to refute was definitional; it was the view that moral properties can be *defined* in non-moral terms. (It is not entirely clear whether the **utilitarians** Moore was criticising held such a view.)

Non-naturalism has been lambasted for cluttering reality with mysterious value-entities or value-properties. In many cases, that assessment may be the result of a hasty and hostile reading of it. The central claim of non-naturalism is that moral properties are not *nothing but* something else, and that they are accessible to cognition. Those claims can be elaborated and explicated without filling reality with mysterious entities or the mind with mysterious faculties.

See **cognitivism, Cudworth, Mackie, Plato**

Further reading: Cudworth 1991; Kant 1976; Moore 1994; Plato 1992

objectivity: This has been interpreted in a number of different ways, but what is shared by the various accounts of objectivity is that ethical considerations are not exhaustively explicated in terms of sensibility, convention, or personal (or group) commitments and conventions. The expression 'ethical considerations' is used broadly here. The objectivist may be arguing that ethical values are objective, that there are ethical facts, that ethical reasons are objective, or that ethical principles are objective. Of course, there are important relations between all of these, but a theorist may be focusing on one rather than the others. For example, **Moore**'s primary concern was to show that ethical values are objective. In recent years, theorists such as Thomas Nagel have argued that ethical reasons are objective. In **Mill**'s **utilitarian** theory there are objective moral facts, namely, facts concerning the utility produced or likely to be produced by different actions or practices. **Plato** argued that Good is an objective reality and that it is an object of intellectual **intuition**. It is not dependent upon what people desire or what they take to be in their interests. **Kant** argued that there are objective moral principles, but he explained their objectivity in terms of the universality and necessity of *a priori* considerations about the form of rational principles of action. He is an example of someone who held that there is moral *objectivity* without moral values being objects. In some accounts there are objective moral reasons, considerations showing actions to be required, permitted, or morally wrong independent of whether agents respond to them as such. Thus, it may be the case that there are reasons for agent A to do X, even if agent A does not consider them or considers them and knowingly fails to act on them.

Critiques and rejections of objectivity come in diverse forms and from several approaches. **Relativists** reject objectivity, and hold that moral values are relative to the norms, beliefs and conventions of groups of people in a way such that no set of them counts as *the* correct or true set of values. Moral sceptics also reject objectivity. **Scepticism** with regard to a given type of entity, property or consideration just is the view that there are no such things as that type. The sceptic may even give an account of morality that is meant to explain it rather than explain it away, but the account will have no place for moral objectivity. (**Hume** can be interpreted as a sceptic of this sort.) Often, critics of objectivity will offer hypotheses about *why* people are moral objectivists. After all, in both the plain person's view and in many philosophical views, objectivity with regard to morality is widely held. This is the approach of **J. L. Mackie** in his formulation of what he calls an '**error theory**'. He tries to show why people are objectivists, even though objectivism is false. It should also be noted that some defenders of objectivity ground it in **divine command** or in God's creating the world order in a way that includes objective moral values and principles. Even if divinely sanctioned morality involves revelation, it has been argued that the morality that is revealed can still be objective. So, a theistic grounding of morality does not automatically render its grounds less or other than objective, at least according to some theistic views.

In general, objectivists hold that moral judgements are **cognitive**; they are literally true or false, rather than their correctness or incorrectness being entirely domesticated to the norms or values that people happen to accept. It is sometimes argued that within a context (i.e. relative to a particular culture or society) moral judgements are objectively correct (or not) given the norms and values of that culture or society. But that is not full-fledged objectivity. Also, objectivity is not the same thing as **absolutism**. The latter is a matter of whether a moral claim or principle or value is universal and not such as ever to be overridden or outweighed. But a claim or principle or value can be objective without being absolute in that sense.

See **subjectivism**

Further reading: Aristotle 1985; Hume 1975 and 1978; Kant 1976; Mackie 1990; Moore 1994; Nagel 1970 and 1986; Plato 1992; Reid 1872; Ross 1930

Open Question Argument: In *Principia Ethica* G. E. Moore developed what he called the 'Open Question Argument'. It was intended to show that any attempt to define a fundamental value (he took good to be the fundamental value) would fail. This could be shown in the following way. Choose any definition or analysis of good you like: for example, suppose we define good as promoting 'the greatest pleasure for the greatest number' or 'what we desire to desire' or 'what most people approve of'. Abbreviate the definition as 'D'. Whatever the content of D, we can ask 'Is D good?' and it is an open question. It is a meaningful, significant question, unlike the question 'Is what we desire to desire what we desire to desire?; 'or, 'Is what promotes the greatest pleasure for the greatest number what promotes the greatest pleasure for the greatest number?' Moore thought he had shown that good is a real, but simple and indefinable object or property. No analysis of it can be given. Moore held that this strategy is a method for showing that the meaning of fundamental value terms cannot be explicated or defined in terms of anything else, whether attitudes, desires, approval, natural or metaphysical facts or properties, and so on. In particular, this was meant by Moore to be part of a destructive critique of naturalism. **Cognitivists** and **realists** welcomed the strategy of the Open Question Argument as supplying an argumentative instrument against **expressivist** interpretations of moral terms. Non-cognitivists and **anti-realists** were impressed by the way the strategy seemed to show that accounts of moral value in terms of natural facts and properties must fail. The Open Question Argument remains important to metaethical theorising because of its focus on the issue of how fact and value are (or are not) related, and on the implications for realism and anti-realism concerning moral value.

See **intuitionism, metaethics, non-naturalism**
Further reading: Frankena 1939; Moore 1994

original position: This is **Rawls**'s notion of a condition in which agents have knowledge of general facts about human nature, interests and propensities, but do not have knowledge of their own particular capabilities, interests and concerns. It is his interpretation of the initial condition in his model of the social **contract** and it is crucial to his procedure for ascertaining principles of justice. The original position is intended to impose a condition of **impartiality** on every agent's consideration of what principles to accept, on the assumption that agents are rational and self-interested (though not in a narrowly **egoist** sense). In this initial situation no one is in a position to fashion principles that would privilege their own situation or abilities, since no one has knowledge of those things. Rawls argued that an initial situation of choice such as this would yield a conception of **justice** as fairness (in contrast to say, justice as to each according to merit, or to each equally, or as maximising **utility**, and so on). This strategy is a recent version of the social contract approach classically developed by early modern thinkers such as **Hobbes, Locke,** and **Rousseau**. It should be noted that while these are all social contract theorists, their for-mulations and approaches differ in significant ways.

See **state of nature, veil of ignorance**

Further reading: Hobbes 1991; Locke 1988; Rawls 1971; Rousseau 1978

particularism: This is the view that moral claims need not, or even cannot be organised into a system of principles or rules that would constitute a codification of moral-ity. Even if (as many particularists would allow) there are important moral general rules, they are arrived at by generalisation from particular cases. One formulation of particularism is that it insists that the moral weight, rel-evance or salience of a consideration in one case may be quite different from its weight, relevance or salience in other cases, even those that are similar in many re-spects. This means that ascertaining what is morally re-quired is a matter of appreciating and comprehending each particular case on the basis of its own highly specific features.

Critics of particularism argue that, of course, judge-ment calibrated to individual cases is necessary, but un-less there are grounds for judgement or moral reasons that are general in scope, there is no way to explain how considerations have the moral significance that they have. For how could conditions in one case have altogether dif-ferent moral weight from what they have in another case? Defenders of particularism can allow that moral general-isations are important in moral learning and in describ-ing key features of situations and actions. However, they will still insist that the moral significance of those fea-tures cannot be captured and expressed first in non-moral terms describing a base upon which moral significance **supervenes**. That is, particularists reject the notion that morality overall can be explicated in terms of invariantly true moral generalisations shown to be true by indicating how moral values supervene on non-moral facts or properties about which we can arrive at those generalisations. Even if the particularist agrees that there are important moral generalisations and principles, he will argue that a correct appreciation of the moral features of any given case depends upon the specific context and features of the case examined holistically, in the particularity of that case. **Aristotle**'s moral epistemology has been interpreted by some as particularist, as have some **intuitionist** moral epistemologies. **Smith** also seems to argue for particularism.

See **practical wisdom, prudence**

Further reading: Aristotle 1985; Dancy 1993; Hooker and Little 2000; McNaughton 1988; Smith 1984

perfectionism: In a perfectionist theory the key valuative notion is that of a fully actualised ideal character or agent. The perfectionist argues that there is an end proper to human nature and that a fully realised or flourishing life, one in which that end is realised and enjoyed, is the fundamental ground of value. The conception of the end might be more or less substantive in the sense that the view involves quite specific **virtues** and activities, rather than being based on the particular agent's choices, interests and concerns. (The individual may have a very flawed conception of what his or her own perfection comprises.) In either case, the key to actualising moral value is well-ordered activity that reflects excellence of character and promotes self-realisation. There need be nothing **egoistic** about this. The fact that perfection of the individual is basic does not imply that agents will or should be interested exclusively in themselves. The well-ordered activity that is perfective may involve virtues that concern our relations with others, such as justice, concern for friends and other people, generosity, and so forth.

Perfectionism includes a **teleological** conception of human nature. It is not necessarily committed to a single superordinate or dominant end, except in the sense that agents are to strive to perfect themselves. A **pluralistic** account of what has worth and what is desirable is compatible with perfectionism. There is an ongoing interpretive debate about whether **Aristotle**'s conception of flourishing (*eudaimonia*) is a conception of a single, highest end or is intended as an inclusive end, constituted by various virtuous activities and commitments to a plurality of values. In either case, his approach to ethics is clearly recognisable as a version of perfectionism.

See **virtue-centred theorising**

Further reading: Aquinas 1966 and 1983; Aristotle 1985; Foot 2001; Hurka 1993; Maimonides 1956 and 1975; Norton 1976

phronesis: See **practical wisdom**.

Plato (427–347 BCE) Greek: Plato's moral theorising fits into a larger, overall conception of reality, value and knowledge. Also, because he wrote nearly all of his works in dialogue form, he does not just directly present his view and the arguments for it. Rather, there is a dialectical process of questioning, teasing out assumptions, raising objections, revising positions, and the like. In reading his works one is drawn into the process of thought through which the views in them are developed. That methodology itself is indicative of something important in Plato's view, namely, that genuine understanding does not come easily and for it to be genuine understanding, one must comprehend the reasons for the true view. Mere possession of correct beliefs is not enough.

This is connected with his view that a rational being is most at home in the world by understanding it. Ignorance, error and illusion are all ways of being alienated from reality, and therefore, lacking a sound comprehension of normative matters. According to Plato, value is real, and it is not grounded in **subjectivity**, will or convention. The good is an object of the understanding, and understanding it is the proper aspiration of a rational being, in order that the person can enact true value in the way she lives. In that way, Plato regarded morality as having to do with the broadest conception of how to lead a life, rather than more narrowly with certain specific obligations.

Justice is at the centre of his interest in this question, and he held that there are important analogies between justice in the individual and justice in the state. In each context there are different elements, capacities and activities that need to be brought into harmony so that the person or the state does not come apart through internal conflict, or conduct her or its activities on the basis of a wrong understanding of what she or it should do and why. Another aspect of the analogy is that there are deep connections between ethics and politics, and that moral education and the cultivation of **virtue** only effectively occur within a social and political order of certain kinds. In both the individual and the state, reason is properly most authoritative. This is because, unlike appetite and spirit (the emotions), reason can form an understanding of the whole and of the best ways for the various parts to be interrelated and functionally to complement each other. In both self-governance and political governance, reason, and in particular, its understanding of justice, is authoritative.

The *Republic* is an extended treatment of how this view is motivated, the main elements of the view, the sort of political order and education required for the cultivation of virtue, and how the virtue of justice is to the good of both the individual and the state. The issue of whether being just is a good to the person who is just, and in what ways it is good, was a matter of paramount concern to Plato. It was at the heart of engagement with questions about what are virtues and why agents should have a concern to acquire them, even when it may disadvantage them in certain ways. The *Republic* is a large-scale, multi-faceted response to the challenge of the **immoralist**, who cannot see why justice is a good to the person who is just, and to the challenge of the **relativist** and conventionalist, who hold that there are no **objective** normative standards and that valuation is not a matter of cognition. Because of the very substantial responsibilities for education and the organisation of social life that Plato assigns to the wise rulers of his ideal state, he has been interpreted as sanctioning a dangerous kind of authoritarianism. At the same time, because of how much is built into the notion of *wise* rulers, he has also been interpreted as a paradigmatic proponent of virtuous governance, guided by a concern for the good of all, informed by an understanding of true values.

Plato wrote extensively about many issues of moral psychology. His works address friendship, **love**, pleasure, desire, self-knowledge, the relations of these in each individual's life, and the relation of these to questions about what is the best kind of life for a human being. His works remain crucial resources for exploration of questions concerning the sources of motivation, the relations between reason and desire, and the role of virtue in an excellent life. Plato's works had considerable influence on medieval Christian thought, the influence being transmitted through neo-Platonists such as **Plotinus**. Some moral realists are Platonists in the respect that they take good to be a real and **non-natural** entity or property, even though their views do not involve the moral psychological elements of

Plato's view and his conception of moral education and the state. **Moore** is an example.

See **Aristotle, Augustine**

Further reading: Moore 1994; Plato 1981 and 1992

Plotinus (205–70 CE) Egyptian or Greek: His thought was a combination of Platonism, **Aristotelianism**, and **Stoic** influence. The Platonic elements of his thought proved to have the most influence, doing much to shape early medieval neo-Platonism. His work, and in particular, his conception of emanation of Intelligence and the Soul, involves a combination of metaphysics and moral psychology in his treatment of some of the main problems **Plato,** and also Christian thinkers, wrestled with. These include the nature of evil and its relation to the Soul, the question of whether evil is a positive reality or a privation of good, and the relation of Intelligence and body in the nature of the Self. He also investigated the question of the nature of **happiness** and whether the person as a composite of body and Soul can attain self-knowledge and happiness.

Further reading: Plotinus 1991

pluralism: One version of pluralism maintains that there is more than one basic moral value or ground of value, and that the different values are irreducible. Accordingly, there are different grounds for various moral principles. For example, the grounds for **autonomy** being a moral value differ from the grounds for mutual benefit being a value. Autonomy and mutual benefit might always be relevant as moral considerations, but not in a way that is exhaustively specified either **a priori** or empirically.

Mill's utilitarianism is an example of value **monism** in that pleasure and pleasure alone is what has value as an end. It is what is to be taken into account in any moral valuation or decision. For **Kant,** the good **will** is the highest good and it alone has unconditioned value, though **happiness** is also a value in that it is desired for its own sake and is part of the 'sole and complete' good (happiness in proportion to virtue). A theory can be mixed in the sense that it acknowledges more than one source of moral value. Care must be taken to indicate as clearly as possible how the values stand in regard to each other, even though the pluralism of the theory rules out the possibility that they are all **commensurable**.

Another version of pluralism holds that there is no single, **objectively** best kind of life, but many good kinds of life. This type of pluralism bears directly on political theory and the question of the appropriate role of the state with respect to conceptions of good, and whether any in particular are to be favoured or encouraged. The pluralist could argue that there are certain constraints on what can count as a good life; for example, there may be certain universally and fundamentally important **virtues**. Still, there could be a great deal of diversity in the specifics of what makes for a good life and what are the virtues that are especially important to this or that kind of life.

See **absolutism, relativism**

Further reading: Nagel 1985; Raz 1986; Williams 1985

practical wisdom: This is an action-guiding **virtue** of thought. The Greek term, transliterated, is *phronesis*. It is especially important in **Aristotle**'s theorising and theorising influenced by him, for example that of **Aquinas**. In **virtue-centred theorising** the virtues of character are dispositional states of desire and the passions, ordered by what reason understands to be good. For instance, courage is a virtue of character concerned with the management of fear. Still, in order to be a full-fledged virtue it must be ordered by a correct conception of what is fearful and what sorts of dangers and risks are worth facing, even at the possible cost of one's life. The virtuous agent needs practical wisdom to be able to ascertain what virtue requires, with respect to overall ends and goods for a human being and with respect to particular situations and possibilities for action.

In theories that endorse the unity of the virtues, practical wisdom is especially important as the virtue needed by all the others so that they are oriented toward what is good. Natural virtues of character dispose an agent in the right way but do not, in their own right, include a conception of what makes those dispositions virtuous. That understanding and the ability to judge and deliberate well require the intellectual dimension of practical wisdom.

In some of **Plato**'s works **Socrates** is portrayed as holding the view that knowledge of the good is sufficient for virtue because no one would knowingly and voluntarily choose what is not good. The differences between the position that knowledge is sufficient for virtue and Aristotle's position is a source of some important debates in moral psychology and moral epistemology. In either view, however, no ethical virtue is perfect or fully present apart from understanding, whether it is held to be sufficient for virtue or only necessary.

See *eudaimonia*, teleology

Further reading: Aquinas 1966 and 1983; Aristotle 1985; Broadie 1991; Hursthouse 1999; Plato 1981 and 1992

preference-utilitarianism: This is a variant of **utilitarianism** according to which actions are evaluated on the basis of how many preferences (weighted to indicate their importance) are satisfied. According to this view, all of a person's ends, interests and values can be translated into the idiom of preferences, and using the criterion of preference-satisfaction is intended to avoid the difficulties of measuring **happiness** and making interpersonal comparisons of it.

See **consequentialism**

Further reading: Singer 1993

prescriptivism: This is an account of moral judgements according to which they are not cognitive, but expressive, and what they express is a command – a prescription for or against the matter at issue. Thus, moral judgements express people's commitments, while those are not reflective of or responsive to **objective** moral considerations. Prescriptivism can be seen as a kind of emotivist **voluntarism**. That is, one's morality reflects choices, while those are not themselves answerable to objective moral considerations. However, prescriptivism also holds that there is a crucial place for **universalisation** in morality. One's prescriptions express moral commitments the agent takes to hold universally. If I claim that 'deliberate inattention to a child's nutritional needs is wrong' I am prescribing against this kind of neglect in a way intended to apply universally rather than just expressing how I happen to feel.

I need to be able to give reasons for thinking this wrong in all cases. One reason might be that such neglect causes needless suffering. But, 'at bottom' those reasons will weigh with me on account of a stance or commitment, rather than a moral fact or a necessarily true rational principle. It is not that 'needless suffering is always morally bad' is objectively true. Rather, I have taken a stand against it, and as a moral stand, I am prescribing it universally. In that regard moral claims differ from claims of merely personal preference (such as taking dark chocolate over milk chocolate or white chocolate).

Prescriptivism integrates considerations of universality with an **expressivist** interpretation of the meaning of moral discourse. Universality is important because of the way in which it reflects something distinctive about moral claims, and the way in which (as a consequence) they involve some formal considerations of rationality. For example, it cannot be permissible for me to do X if it is impermissible for you to do it, if the conditions are similar. And, different prescriptions need to be consistent with each other.

See **anti-realism, emotivism, Hare**
Further reading: Hare 1963 and 1973

Prichard, H. A. (1871–1947) English: He was an **intuitionist** who held that there are self-evident, simple moral properties, among which obligatoriness is fundamental. As an intuitionist his moral epistemology was similar to **Moore's**, though they disagreed over what property it is that is intuited. (Moore argued that it is **good**.) Prichard argued that any attempt to give an analysis of obligatoriness or to give a reductionist explication of it is bound to fail. It is a simple, unique property we can directly apprehend. Moreover, according to Prichard, we do not need to provide an extra-moral motive or interest to be moral. Moral obligatoriness has stand-alone status. To explicate it in any other way, or to explain how it can be motivating because of how it is supported by some non-moral consideration would misrepresent the (intuitively self-evident) nature of obligatoriness.

See **anti-realism, deontology, Kant, realism, Ross**
Further reading: Prichard 1912

prima facie: **W. D. Ross** used the expression '*prima facie*' to refer to the obligations inherent in moral considerations prior to the point at which a judgement, all things considered, is reached. For example, one has a *prima facie* obligation to do X if one has promised to do so. However, some other obligation may override that one, as events unfold. Stopping to aid people urgently in need of help may take priority over fulfilling the promise. '*Prima facie*' does not indicate that the obligation is weak or merely apparent. Ross used the expression in order to indicate the difference between something being obligatory in its own right, and what is obligatory once all of the relevant moral features are taken into account. It was an important part of his view that we should take into account the larger context or situation in ascertaining what indeed, are our obligations in the case. Through **intuition** we can recognise *prima facie* obligations. It is through careful attention to actual circumstances that we determine precisely what we are to do.

Further reading: Ross 1930

projectivism: This is a **metaethical** position that holds that moral value is not independent of affect, stances or attitudes that we project onto things. Moral value is not 'there' apart from our responses and concerns. While this is a version of **subjectivism,** it need not be committed to the claim that because moral value is projected it is less than fully genuine. The projectivist may claim to give an account of the status of moral value rather than explaining it away or concluding that there is none. **Hume** can be interpreted as a projectivist of this 'explaining, but not explaining away' sort. The projectivist might concede that if projectivism is true then moral judgements are not literally true or false in the realist's sense, but may also argue that that is not a condition for the authority of moral considerations and the significance of moral judgements. Acceptance of projectivism does not in its own right restrict one's first-order moral theory with regard to what it takes to be right, wrong, permissible, obligatory, and so on. That, it can be argued, is a matter *within* morality and not a second-order issue.

See **anti-realism, Blackburn, expressivism, realism**
Further reading: Blackburn 1993 and 1998; Hume
1975 and 1978

prudence: In some ethical theories 'prudence' is a term for
practical wisdom; for the action-guiding **virtue** of thought
through which the agent understands the good. In a different conception of prudence a consideration is a prudential
consideration if it concerns the agent's own good in contrast to the welfare of others or what is owed to them.
In that use prudence is contrasted with **altruism** (whether
or not altruism involves sentiments such as **benevolence**
or **sympathy**). In many versions of contract theorising, it
is prudence that motivates individuals to participate in a
social **contract** through which they might surrender some
of their rights in the **state of nature** in order to secure
liberties and security in a civil order.

'Prudence' is often understood as something like 'reflective, or considered rational self-interest'. That is not
to say that a prudent agent is narrowly self-interested or
an **egoist**. Rather, the prudent agent considers his own
interests as having significant weight not automatically
overidden by altruistic considerations. Indeed, in some
theories it is prudence that motivates agents to accept
moral obligations insofar as their interests are best served
by participating in a moral order. When prudence is interpreted as practical wisdom, prudent activity is in their
interest in a different sense. It is through practically wise
activity that they most fully realise or actualise human
good, and thus lead a flourishing life. Prudent activity
is a good to the prudent agent, however, the practically
wise agent is aiming at what is fine or just, and not at
self-interest narrowly construed.

See **Aquinas, Aristotle, Plato, virtue-centred theorising**
Further reading: Aquinas 1966 and 1983; Aristotle
1985; Foot 1978 and 2001; Hursthouse 1999; Plato 1992

Pufendorf, Samuel von (1632–94) German: A **natural law** theorist, Pufendorf attempted to combine the demonstrative rigour of Cartesianism with the emerging empiricism of the age, in an attempt to put law, the fundamentals of political theory, and jurisprudence on a scientific basis. In that respect, he is important for developing a conception of natural law that departed from the scholastic model. He regarded natural law as comprising both religious and rational principles, and he understood the state and state power in terms of a **Hobbes**-influenced conception of the rule of law. He was also influenced by **Grotius**.

Further reading: Pufendorf 1991

punishment: Issues concerning the justification of punishment and questions about how to proportion punishments to offences are long-standing matters of philosophical disagreement. Justifications of several kinds have been offered. For **retributivists** the key consideration is desert. In that view the fact of being guilty of wrongdoing is a necessary condition of punishment and a sufficient condition. Retributivists need to explicate *why* this is the case. In some of the most influential retributivist accounts (such as **Kant** and **Hegel's**) punishment is explicated as being brought on the offender by his own action. Justice requires that the wrongdoer submit to principles of desert that his own rational nature endorses (Kant) or to the annulling of his offence, acknowledging punishment as the rational response to his action as an attack upon freedom and reason (Hegel). Some retributivists (e.g. Kant) argue that if punishment is merited, there is an obligation to impose it; it is not merely permitted, it is an obligation.

Consequentialist theories typically appeal to considerations of deterrence, and sometimes also to correction as the main justifying grounds. Most consequentialists will include the retributivist condition that only offenders are to be punished, but they may try to do this on consequentialist grounds. (How much confidence would there be in a justice system that officially sanctioned punishing anyone known to be innocent?) The consequentialist will argue that unless punishment does some good; unless it brings a benefit that cannot be obtained by any less harmful means, it is not justified. (**Bentham** and **Mill** are key examples.) Consequences may include such factors as the effective disincentive to potential offenders, the increased safety of law-abiding persons, and the confidence of the community that there is an effective criminal justice system. To the extent that punishment does not make a positive causal difference (of those, and possibly other kinds) it lacks justification. This helps explain why consequentialists often argue for less severe punishments than retributivists might endorse. However, it is important to note that retributivism does not necessarily endorse especially severe punishments. The main consideration is that the most grave offences merit the most severe punishments. But that does not automatically mean 'the most severe punishments we can think of'.

There are also justifications of punishment in terms of its expressive function. This is the view that it expresses or communicates denunciation, in a way that a fine, for example, does not. In that respect it is a way for a society to indicate the genuineness and significance of its commitment to certain values and norms. Another communicative role sometimes attributed to punishment is that it is a way of respecting the offender as a rational agent, and the punishment is intended to help the offender acknowledge his wrong and motivate him ethically to self-correct. The project of ethical self-correction is important in views (such as **Plato**'s) that justify punishment as a manner of promoting the psychic health; the well-being of the person punished. In that respect, punishment may be painful but it is not harming. Any practice that is meant to harm, or that only harms without improving the person who suffers it, is unjustified.

There are eclectic or mixed views that include elements from two or more different approaches, and 'pure' views of one or another kind are the exception rather than the rule. Also, some theorists distinguish between the aims of punishment and the justification of it. This might be because they want to distinguish between what normatively grounds it and what difference it makes. Understandably, consequentialists will often refer to the 'justifying aims' of punishment, because the difference it makes is crucial to its normative ground. As noted above, in addition to the questions of justification there are questions about what punishments are appropriate to specific offences.

See **justice**

Further reading: Hegel 1981; Kant 1965; Mill 1979; Plato 1994

rationalism: A moral rationalist gives an account of moral requirements on the basis of reason's capacity to be epistemically authoritative. The rationalist argues that there is a principle or set of principles which can be ascertained by rational reflection and shown to be essential to moral evaluation and moral reasoning. Reason, unaided by sensibility or desire, can achieve conceptions of what is permitted, required and prohibited. That kind of explication and justification is, according to the rationalist, necessary for morality. It also shows how moral considerations can move moral agents, in that those considerations have motivational efficacy insofar as agents are rational. The rationalist approach to moral theorising is the project of showing that reason on its own is adequate for supplying substantive rules of action, moral duties incumbent upon us as rational agents.

See *a priori*, **deontology, Kant, naturalism**

Further reading: Donagan 1977; Gert 1966; Kant 1976

Rawls, John (1921–2002) American: In *A Theory of justice* Rawls made a case for liberal political theory based upon a conception of **justice** as fairness, and he supplied an account of how to ascertain the fundamental principles of justice. That work and his subsequent revisions and development of his view have been very influential in recent political philosophy and also in ethics. The main significance of his work for ethics is his methodology for determining what principles and obligations rationally self-interested agents would agree to, conceptualising those agents in an 'original position' behind a 'veil of ignorance' This is how the conception of justice as fairness, arrived at in a way that ensures **impartiality**, is explicated. There are some pronounced **Kantian** features in his view (e.g. the importance of respecting each person as a free and equal participant in the moral order). However, Rawls's approach was a version of **coherentism** elaborated in terms of 'reflective equilibrium' rather than based on principles of pure practical reason. He does not rely on the metaphysical conception of rational agency crucial to Kant. Moral principles are constructed in ways that all rational agents can accept, and **objectivity** can be attained in that way rather than by appeal to purported moral facts. The view overall, and particularly with regard to politics, is a version of **contract theory**.

See **autonomy, deontology, natural rights, rights, state of nature**

Further reading: Gauthier 1986; Kant 1965 and 1976; Rawls 1971; Williams 1981

realism: The realism/**anti-realism** debate occurs in many areas of philosophy and there are different ways to characterise this. In some views, realism is the position that holds that some specific type of entity or feature (such as the wrongness of an action or the goodness of a state of affairs) exists. In other views, it is taken to be the position that statements of certain kinds (such as moral statements) are literally true or false. Each of these approaches makes for the **objectivity** of ethics, the first focusing on what there is (ontology) and the latter focusing on the semantic issue of truth-evaluability. The anti-realist, in either case, denies what the realist asserts, and offers an explanation of those features and of the status of statements about them without the realist's metaphysical and/or semantic commitments. Moreover, one can be a realist in one disputed area without being a realist in others. For example, a realist about the entities referred to in scientific theories is not thereby committed to moral or aesthetic realism.

In the context of ethics, realism is the view that there are moral values or properties that are not fully grounded in or dependent upon sensibility, desire, interest or choice; they are not projected onto the world. That is why moral claims are literally true or false. They are not be interpreted expressively, as being correct or not strictly in terms of norms and criteria grounded in wants, concerns and responses, and not objectively evaluable. There are versions of anti-realism according to which moral discourse has all the form of realist discourse, but in fact does not refer to objective values or have realist truth-conditions. Versions of that type are not intended to undermine the significance of moral thought and judgement. They are meant to explain that significance without realist commitments. There are other versions of anti-realism that are indeed intended to show that moral discourse cannot have the significance we tend to attribute to it.

Likewise, there are many versions of realism. **Plato** is a paradigmatic realist and **Aristotle, Mill** and **Moore** are also realists, though their conceptions of the nature of moral reality differ in important ways. Moore, for example, is a **non-naturalist** realist, while Mill is a **naturalist** realist. **Kant** held that moral judgements are objectively correct or mistaken and thus he is a **cognitivist** though he is not a realist in any of the ways in which the above-mentioned thinkers are. It is possible to interpret Kant as a realist, though Kantian realism is not grounded in the mind-independent reality of moral entities or properties. It is grounded in the rational *construction* of moral requirements. In being independent of sensibility and in being unconditioned by anything external to pure practical reason (at least in Kant's own view) it could be said that the view is a realist one. The requirements of practical reason yield moral imperatives that are universal and necessary. Still, there is a role for rational construction that differentiates the view from most realist accounts. Most of the recent defences of realism have not involved theological considerations, but the view that moral truths are grounded in God's will can also be a version of realism. It still faces the **Euthyphro problem,** but **divine command** realism may be an example of realist voluntarism, while in non-theistic theories, realists tend to contrast their positions with **voluntarism.** It should also be kept in mind that the interpretation of realism is itself a contested matter. In addition to the realist/anti-realist debate there are significant, ongoing philosophical disputes about what exactly each of them is committed to.

See **emotivism, expressivism, intuitionism, prescriptivism**

Further reading: Aristotle 1985; Ayer 1952; Blackburn 1993 and 1998; Kant 1976; McDowell 1988 and 1997; Mill 1979; Moore 1994; Plato 1992; Platts 1979

reflective equilibrium: Whether in ethics or in other contexts, this is a method aimed at maximising the overall coherence of both particular judgements on the one hand and general principles and theoretical claims on the other. The role of it in ethics has been highlighted by **Rawls**'s *A Theory of Justice*. In that work it is the method by which we are to ascertain the fundamental principles of justice that would be approved by rational agents in a project of fashioning a social **contract**. In aiming at reflective equilibrium no claims have a **foundational** status. There can be adjustments to particular judgements and to theoretical claims in striving for enhanced coherence. The overall system of cohering beliefs is such that our considered judgements conform with our principles as a result of critical reflection upon them and the relations between them.

See **original position**

Further reading: Rawls 1971

regret: Regret is important in moral theorising because of how it is related to self-determination, voluntariness, **fortune**, and moral self-knowledge. There are many things that we regret even though we had no role in them. We regret that the tornado ruined the orchard, or that the heavy traffic made us arrive late. But there is also regret that we often feel with respect to situations in which we were agents, though what is bad or awful about them was not directly traceable to our agency or intentions. Suppose you are looking after a neighbour's child at a playground, and you help the child to the top of a slide, and while the child is there, the structure buckles and collapses because of long-accumulating rust and poor maintenance. You certainly had no intention to endanger or harm the child, and you are not responsible for what went wrong; but it would seem very odd and probably disturbing for you simply to think, 'Accidents happen, and it looks like this kid's number was up. It's not my fault and I'm not going to beat myself up over it'. What most of us expect as at least part of the proper reaction is regret over your role in the situation though you did not voluntarily cause the harm. There is some respect in which your agency in the case is a source of pain to you, even though the harm was not intended. There are many kinds of cases in which we feel regret with regard to our agency even though our intentions are above reproach, and we were attentive to circumstances. Still, the regret is much stronger if it is a child who falls with the collapse of the slide, instead of a toy car that we put at the top of it. It is not bad luck that we regret; it is our having been an agent in the situation though the harm was caused involuntarily. It may be morally appropriate to feel more regret over success at committing a murder than at the attempt without success but the latter should not be free of regret just because no one died.

Questions of the relation between the non-voluntary and the regrettable, and the relation between intention and outcome centrally involve questions about regret as an issue of moral psychology and as a factor that figures in our moral judgements of agents and actions.

Further reading: Aristotle 1985; Nagel 1985; Statman 1993; Williams 1981

Reid, Thomas (1710–96) Scottish: Reid's main importance in ethics is his defence of moral **objectivity** and moral **cognitivism** against approaches such as **Hume**'s. Reid argued that in moral judgement we are not merely expressing stances or feelings; we are asserting propositions. The various acts of moral judgement, including condemning, acquitting, excusing, accusing and so on, involve feelings, but the feelings are not themselves the bases of the judgements. Indeed, feeling may follow judgement, and we are able to distinguish between the object of judgement and the act of mind by which we judge. Feeling does not involve that distinction. There is, in Reid's view, a moral faculty, the existence of which is evident, and there are principles of morality that we can know to be true by the exercise of that faculty. Reid's work (overall, not just as regards morality) had a good deal of influence in his time, and its influence then waned. In recent years there has been a considerable increase of interest in Reid and his thought is more visibly figuring in current debates in moral epistemology and in other areas as well.

See **expressivism, intuitionism, subjectivism**

Further reading: Reid 1872

relativism: This is the view that the correctness or validity of ethical claims depends upon norms, commitments and circumstances that are not grounds for **objective** rightness or wrongness. This does not mean that 'anything goes'. It means that what is permitted, required and prohibited, and how actions and agents are morally evaluated, are relative to cultural contexts. Relativists often note that different societies and different times have different conceptions of what is morally right and wrong, and different conceptions of **virtue** and of the things meriting praise and blame. Also, relativists sometimes argue that if there were **objective** values or objective moral considerations, would not there be more agreement in judgement than there is? However, the case for relativism needs to show that there is no objective moral reality, not just that there are some striking differences in moral belief and practice. The key issue is whether there is something for moral thought to converge on, not whether there are, in fact, disagreements. In addition, the relativist can be pressed to specify what are the relevant groups or contexts to which moral considerations are relative. Any person belongs to many groups (national, ethnic, religious, linguistic, occupational, geographic, historical, and so on). What are the appropriate groups with reference to which we should be examining the relativity of morality? That issue might be somewhat defused if the relativist has already made a strong case for **non-cognitivism**.

It can be helpful to distinguish relativism from **pluralism**. The pluralist position that there are different, irreducible values is compatible with moral objectivity. The diversity of value *per se* is not indicative of relativism. Also, it can be helpful to examine the relation between relativism and **subjectivism**. It may be that one can be a subjectivist without being a relativist if it can be shown that the best account of moral values is one in which they are subjective, but also universal. It depends upon what is taken to be the basis for the subjectivity of values.

Further reading: Harman 1977; Mackie 1990; Williams 1972; Wong 1984

respect: In many moral theories persons are regarded as having a distinct status such that they are owed a distinct kind of regard. This is not respect for their talents, achievements, or the means at their disposal, such as wealth or influence. Rather, it is respect owed to each person as a self-determining rational agent and an equal participant in a common moral order. This moral respect is central in **Kant**'s theorising and in many accounts of persons' rights. A violation of a **right** is sometimes interpreted as a failure of respect, or as using a person merely as a means. Typically, rationality is the basis for this respect, in contrast to say, morally owing things to persons on account of the fact that they can experience pleasure and pain. There might be things that are desirable for their own sake and thus significant to a theory of value, while being independent of the type of respect indicated here. Critics of **consequentialist** moral theories sometimes object to them on the grounds that they fail to respect adequately persons as distinct individuals. A consequentialist may insist that each person is to count equally, but the moral worth of actions and practices is still to be ascertained on the basis of consequences rather than fixed or unrevisable limits on how persons are to be treated.

See **autonomy**

Further reading: Hill 1991; Kant 1976; Rawls 1971

retributivism: This is a position with regard to the justification of **punishment**. The retributivist holds that guilt (the fact, not the feeling) is both necessary and sufficient for punishment to be justified, even though this on its own does not resolve the issue of just *what* the punishment should be. For the retributivist, the main consideration in the justification of punishment is that the wrongdoer deserves to be punished whatever else might be among the aims of punishment. If punishing offenders has a deterrent effect on others, or if it motivates offenders to self-correct ethically, those are very welcome outcomes, but they are not elements of the moral grounds for punishment. Retributive punishment is not the same thing as revenge. The latter is typically motivated by passion and it aims at harming the offender, perhaps along with gratifying the revenge-taker.

Retributivism's main concern is **justice**. Of course, other approaches to justifying punishment also regard justice as crucial, but they take considerations of the sorts mentioned above into account as well. Most approaches include the retributivist constraint that only offenders are to be punished, but for them that is one condition among many. Retributivists often insist that justice also requires that punishments should be fitting; proportional to the gravity of offences. This does not require capital punishment for murder, or corporal punishment for assault, and so forth. Rather, the most grave offences merit the most severe punishments. Whether those latter could include the death penalty, life imprisonment, sentences without parole, and so on, is a hotly debated issue.

Kant came closest to developing a 'pure' retributivism, and one in which capital punishment is not only permitted, but in some cases, required. He also held that failure to punish wrongdoers is a second offence. There are many retributivists who depart from him on those matters, but still regard his view that punishment is required by justice – it is justified by considerations of desert – as crucial. In most retributivist theories of punishment the basis of desert is that we are rational agents, capable of acting for reasons and on principles that we endorse. As such we are accountable for our actions, and we merit reward and punishment for that reason.

See **consequentialism**

Further reading: Hampton and Murphy 1998; Hart 1995; Hegel 1981; Kant 1965

rights: This is a large and complex sphere of moral theorising. Some of the most basic issues are these: (1) What fundamental kinds of rights are there? Are there natural or moral rights in addition to legal rights?; (2) If there are natural (or moral) rights, what precisely is their ground?; (3) How do we ascertain what are properly people's rights? Even if we simply say that 'rights are what the law says they are' we still need a rationale for taking that view and for regrading some legally positivistic conceptions of rights as correct and others as incorrect; (4) Positive rights would be rights *to do* or *to have* something. Negative rights are rights of non-interference, rights *not* to be impeded in doing or having something. They are rights that impose constraints on what agents may permissibly do in ways that affect others. Are there positive and negative rights, or rights of just one type?; (5) How do rights stand with respect to other moral considerations? Is there a defensible general principle concerning the issue of whether rights override other considerations?; (6) If there are natural or moral rights, do they concern a distinct status and inviolability of persons, or do they concern certain interests of persons, or both?

There are moral theories in which rights are fundamental. This is true of **Hobbes, Locke,** and **Kant**'s conceptions of morality. The former two argued that the **natural rights** of persons are the data which supply a basis upon which a social contract and legitimate political authority can be built. Kant held that rational agents simply as such are owed a distinct kind of respect, and thus have the right never to be treated merely as means. In more recent theorising there has been extensive discussion of what positive rights persons have, for example concerning equality of opportunities, the fulfilling of basic needs and for education, health care, and so on. The early modern discussion of rights tended to focus on the requirement of political authority to protect individuals' rights. That was certainly true of classical liberalism, which said little about what society should provide beyond protecting negative rights.

Further reading: Dworkin 1977; Grotius 2004; Hobbes 1991; Kant 1965; Locke 1988; Mill 1979; Rawls 1971

Ross, W. D. (1877–1940) English: Ross was an **intuitionist** who introduced the notion of '*prima facie*' obligations. These are obligations that one can recognise as self-evidently so, unless other moral considerations override them. This was a way of retaining the notion of some moral requirements being intuitively **foundational** while also acknowledging that the particular features of different cases may make a difference to what is morally required all things considered. His intuitionism differed from **Moore**'s in that Ross held that various moral duties are known intuitively rather than the single object, good, being known intuitively. Thus, rightness as well as goodness is a fundamental category of morality. In addition, Ross made it quite clear that the self-evidence of the right and the good does not mean that it is obvious what is right or good. One may need a good deal of experience and conceptual fluency to do well at moral judgement and decision, and in many cases there may be numerous relevant moral considerations that are related in complex ways.

See **Cambridge Platonists, objectivity, Prichard**
Further reading: Ross 1930

Rousseau, J. J. (1712–78) Swiss: He is a key figure in the Romanticist critique of Enlightenment rationalism, and important for his overall philosophical anthropology. Rousseau's presence in ethics is largely through *The Social Contract*, a work that offered a radically different conception of man's natural state and its relation to the civil condition. Unlike **Hobbes** and **Locke** (and many others) Rousseau presented the natural state of man – the condition of a noble savage – as corrupted by the development of the competition, vanity, the rule of laws that institutionalise injustice, competitive self-interest and the like, that are features of humanity's social (as opposed to natural) condition. The social, civil world is something of a fall from innocence and not an unmixed improvement over the state of nature. Human freedom is restricted and restrained in civil society and it inevitably brings inequalities (and all of their attendant abuses) in its train. However, it is also the basis for the development of civic virtues and the cultivation of a new sort of freedom in which each can understand her individual will as in harmony with the wills of other participants in the civic order. This is the rational, self-conscious freedom of political association in which sovereignty is grounded in the general will. Unity with others through the general will is (Rousseau thought) a way of overcoming alienation and a way to reconstruct human freedom so that it no longer brings inequality and undemocratic relations of power and domination. This is in some respects a forerunner of **Kant**'s notion of rational self-legislation as the basis for morality and the fundamental principles of political right.

See **social contract, state of nature**

Further reading: Rousseau 1978

rule-utilitarianism: This version of **utilitarianism** holds that in determining what is to be done, we should be guided by our understanding of which rules and practices have the best record of maximising utility when followed. The view contrasts with **act-utilitarianism**. The rule-utilitarian argues that there is greater utility in following rules than in examining individual acts as the basis for ascertaining what to do, even if doing so may sometimes lead to individual actions that do not maximise utility. The rule-utilitarian concedes that there may be some cases in which dishonesty would bring the most utility, but overall – and taking into account the utility involved in trying to figure out what to do – there is a decisive case for honesty. Thus, we should encourage the habit of honesty as a completely general approach to communication and representation. What we need to justify are general rules or practices, and then individual acts will be justified or not, given how they stand with respect to the rules and practices. The rule-utilitarian will claim to be true to utilitarianism because of the purported overall utility of relying on rules in certain ways.

See **Mill**

Further reading: Bentham 1996; Lyons 1965; Mill 1979; Smart and Williams 1973; Williams 1972

$\boxed{\text{S}}$

Sartre, Jean-Paul (1905–80) French: Sartre has standing as a
philosopher, novelist and public intellectual. He wrote on
a wide range of philosophical topics and his work on the
nature of freedom, radical choice, and the accompanying
responsibility bears most directly on ethics. The notion
that we are responsible for our choices and our values –
and that we are not to explain what we do and what we
endorse on the basis of factors external to us – is a central
theme of his work. Freedom is problematic for us because
on the one hand, we look to reason or nature (principles
or facts or causes) to govern or guide it, while on the other,
we are aware of ourselves as free, as being the origins
and authors of our choices, including whatever criteria
for choices we might appeal to. That is just what freedom is. Human consciousness is a meaning-conferring
activity, not a 'thing', and in leading a life one must take
responsibility for the meaning one confers upon things.
It is in that capacity to consider itself, while also realising
that it is not a 'thing' or an object with a fixed nature,
that human consciousness attains a sense of its uniqueness
and the uniqueness of the human predicament. Human
nature is neither rationally nor naturalistically fixed, nor
determined to have an essence. Our lives are projects of
radical choice, for which we are responsible, no matter
how determined we are to find a basis for choice and
value in rational or natural necessity. Sartre is one of the
most important **existentialist** thinkers.
    See **Kierkegaard, Nietzsche**
    Further reading: Sartre 1947

scepticism: There are several different variants of scepticism.
    In general, scepticism with regard to morality is a
    view that denies that there are **objective** moral values

and denies that there are literally true or false moral judgements. Judgements may be correct insofar as they accord with prevailing norms or principles, but there are no objective bases for the norms and principles. A sceptic need not be a **nihilist**, denying that there is morality or moral value at all. Scepticism is most often directed at claims about the status of moral value and moral claims without necessarily being part of a case against the reality and significance of morality. In moral theorising, as in other contexts, sceptical challenges to claims about what there is and how we can have knowledge of it are very important. Claims for the objectivity or **realism** of moral values are often held to be especially problematic because knowledge of them would need to be action-guiding. How could knowledge – understanding that something is the case – move us to act in addition to believing? There are moral theorists who are sceptics concerning realist conceptions of moral value, but not sceptics concerning morality. They hold that **subjectivist** bases are adequate to account for moral judgement and moral motivation. **Hume** holds a view of that kind.

See **amoralism, Mackie, metaethics, naturalism, rationalism**

Further reading: Hume 1975 and 1978; Mackie 1990; Moore 1994

Scotus, Duns (c. 1265–1308) Scottish: Scotus is an important figure in several areas of philosophy, but his importance in ethics has to do with his articulation and defence of a voluntaristic conception of morality, grounded in divine **will**. The controversy concerning **voluntarism** involved the question of whether morality is knowable through reason and its comprehension of **natural law**, or whether it has a ground and obligatoriness elsewhere, for example in God's will. Scotus argued for the latter position, regarding it as necessary to preserve God's freedom. If divine volition is constrained by rational requirements (other than respecting the law of non-contradiction) that would be a restriction on God's freedom and power. Scotus allowed that there are moral requirements that can be known through reason, given the world-order that God has created, with things having the natures they have. However, God could have made different natures, for which there would be different moral requirements. Even given the natures of things in the actual world, at least some moral requirements could have been different, had God willed it. Moreover, even for those requirements with a basis in natural law, it is the fact that God has willed those natures to be governed by those laws that makes following natural law obligatory. The naturalness of the laws does not also fully ground our obligation to act in accord with them. The ground for that is obedience to God.

See **Aquinas, William of Ockham**
Further reading: Scotus 1987

Sidgwick, Henry (1838–1900) English: In *The Methods of Ethics* Sidgwick presented an extensive articulation and analysis of what he took to be the most fundamental approaches to moral theory, and his account has proved to be of lasting significance, especially with regard to the assessment of **utilitarianism**. The three approaches that he took to be fundamental are (1) **intuitionism**; (2) egoistic **hedonism**; and (3) universalistic hedonism (utilitarianism). The intuitionist holds that certain moral judgements are self-evident, known to be true without being based upon any other considerations, including the consequences of actions. For example one might hold that 'it is morally wrong to demean someone who has helped and supported you' is intuitively evident. **Egoistic** hedonism is the view that each person ought to maximise his own **happiness,** understood as pleasurable experiences or states of consciousness. Universalistic hedonism is the view that what one morally ought to do is to maximise happiness overall, without any special regard to one's own happiness.

Sidgwick presented a highly detailed and rigorous account of these approaches, how they stand with respect to common sense moral judgement, and why they are the most fundamental approaches. His account includes discussions of self-love, **virtue, justice,** and various duties, among other things. He concluded that the case for hedonism is stronger than the case for intuitionism. However, the case for hedonism (whether egoistic or universalistic) ultimately depends upon an intuitive judgement that happiness is intrinsically good. To that extent, there is not total independence from intuition. Still, the matter of which specific moral rules and judge-ments are correct depends upon the hedonist method in that they depend upon consideration of the amount of happiness that will be brought about. Yet, Sidgwick was not able to ascertain conclusively and systematically whether egoistic hedonism or universalistic hedonism should prevail. It is clear, he thought, that happiness is the good, but it is not clear whether one ought always to act so as to maximise one's own good, or to act so as to maximise the good overall. Indeed, the egoist may quite coherently wonder whether there *is* a good overall, and it is quite understandable that one's concern for one's own good is different from one's concern with the good of others. Yet, it is also clear that if there is a good overall, then one ought to seek to maximise it, since one's own good is simply one small element of it. In the end, there is no clear case for the one method over the other.

Sidgwick's treatment of these issues provided an especially exhaustive account of utilitarianism and the grounds for it, as well as a clear articulation of some of the most basic and unavoidable problems of moral theorising and their relation to common sense judgements.

See **Bentham, Mill, Moore**

Further reading: Sidgwick 1981

Singer, Peter (1946–) Australian: He is a contemporary philosopher who has argued extensively for **utilitarianism** and also for animal **rights**. Holding that **intrinsic value** resides in states of consciousness or experience, Singer makes the case that there is nothing essentially different about human beings that sets them a moral status distinct from that of other creatures capable of experiencing pleasure and pain. He has extended his approach to several specific moral matters such as **euthanasia,** abortion and infanticide. In each case he has argued in favour of them in ways that have aroused considerable controversy. He defends a version of **preference utilitarianism,** according to which actions are evaluated on the basis of whether they satisfy the most preferences, weighted by the strength of those preferences. This approach is intended to avoid some of the difficulties involved in the measurement of how much pleasure is experienced by different subjects and the difficulties of interpersonal comparisons of experiences of pleasure.

See **consequentialism**

Further reading: Singer 1981 and 1993

Smith, Adam (1723–90) Scottish: One of the main figures among the British moralists, Smith's conception of the 'impartial spectator' continues to figure prominently in contemporary debates in moral epistemology. Smith sought to show that sentiments are the basis for moral judgements, at the same time that the device of the impartial spectator enables individuals to bring their judgements into agreement with what would be approved by observers. Also a Scot, his life substantially overlapped with Hume's. Like **Hume,** Smith takes **sympathy** to be crucial to morality, but it is sympathy construed broadly as the ability to have fellow-feeling with another person's passions, whatever they are. Sympathy is not equated with compassion or pity. While Smith grounds moral judgement in the sentiments, this is not a version of **emotivism.** Taking the view of the impartial spectator enables an agent to assess and even revise his sentiments with a view to their meriting approval. The impartial spectator is our **conscience,** through which we are able to ascertain whether or not our judgements meet standards of **virtue.** There are **Stoic** elements as well in Smith's theory, especially with regard to the importance of self-command and propriety. We are to try to judge ourselves as others see us, and this often involves restraining passions and tempering attitudes in ways that guard against indulgent self-concern.

See **ideal observer**

Further reading: Smith 1984

sociobiology: This is a strategy of explanation aimed at accounting for social behaviour, including human behaviour, in biological terms, with a central role being accorded to the theory of evolution. Genetics, facts about adaptation, and ecological considerations are involved in sociobiological accounts. Sociobiologists are especially interested in **altruistic** behaviour because of how it seems to be at odds with the individual agent's own survival. If it can be shown to be adaptive, that would be an important element of a sociobiological account of its persistence. Critics often charge that sociobiological hypotheses and explanations are so plastic that they can be adjusted to account for whatever behavioural phenomenon is in question. In a certain sense, there is always *some* biological basis for behaviour. We are organisms and we would not have the capacities and propensities we have without the genetic code we have. Sociobiologists counter by arguing that the sensibility, basic strategies of action, and the social relations between people that are so crucial to morality can be shown to be not just consistent with evolution by natural selection, but substantively explained by it (along with the other considerations mentioned above). In that respect, sociobiology is a version of **naturalism**.

See **evolutionary ethics**

Further reading: Huxley 1989; Wilson 1978

Socrates (c. 470–399 BCE) Greek: Best known through the portrayal of him in many of Plato's dialogues, Socrates left no writings of his own while having an enormous impact on philosophy and the conception of philosophy. His relentless concern to question beliefs and to challenge intellectual and moral complacency, without claiming to have the truth about the matters in question, remains a model of philosophical method and the philosophical life.

With respect to ethics in particular, Socrates's dialectical moves focused on the question of what **virtue** is, whether it can be taught, the role of knowledge in virtue, and the relation of virtue to a well-led life. He is portrayed defending the theses that corrupting someone is the worst harm that can be done to a person, that knowledge is sufficient for virtue, that the virtues are unified, and that no one acts wrongly voluntarily; wrong actions are explicable by ignorance rather than deliberate wrongfulness. **Plato** was strongly influenced by Socrates, and Platonic dialectic philosophical method is one of the most evident results of that influence. In Socratic method there is a combination of rigorously pursuing truth while assiduously avoiding dogmatism. In particular, Plato wrestled with the Socratic theses concerning whether knowledge is sufficient for virtue, and whether **justice** (or virtue overall) is a good to the just person.

Socrates was tried and convicted for the offences of being impious and corrupting the youth of Athens. He was widely known for raising and pursuing questions that raised doubts (and the accompanying defensiveness and awkwardness) among Athenians, motivating them to examine the bases of their convictions, and often showing that they could not. His questioning exposed weaknesses in the prevailing views and made for a sharp contrast with the **Sophists**' method of educating young people in methods and strategems of argument that would help them be victorious disputants, but without regard to truth. The Sophists worked for pay while Socrates saw his project as something quite different from a paying job. In *Crito* Socrates argues against his friends that he ought to obey the laws of the city that has condemned him, because of what he owes to the city, in spite of the erroneous grounds of his conviction. Many of the main problems in ethics and politics and their points of contact with each other are motivated and formulated by Socrates in Plato's dialogues. **Aristotle** referred to Socrates with respect even though he was critical of Socrates's and Plato's views.

Further reading: Plato 1981 and 1992

Sophists: 'Sophists' refers to a number of Greek thinkers in the fifth and fourth centuries BCE. Some of them, such as Protagoras and Thrasymachus, figure prominently in some of Plato's dialogues. The Sophists made their living as teachers, instructing others in how to win arguments and how to be persuasive, how to succeed, whatever the issue or the side of the issue one is on. They and their rhetorical strategies were the object of considerable criticism on **Socrates's** part. Various Sophists claimed to be able to teach **virtue**. Sophists also advocated a version of moral **relativism** and some held the view that **justice** is conventional and that often there are advantages in being unjust even if there is a point in appearing to be just. These are at the heart of **Socrates** and **Plato**'s concerns. Indeed, the Sophists are important for having formulated some of the most basic and enduring moral issues.

Further reading: Plato 1992 and 1994

Spinoza, Benedictus de (1632–77) Dutch: Spinoza was a systematic thinker and his views of ethics reflect the overall system and method of his thought. His metaphysical views are the grounding of his ethics, and both his metaphysics and his ethics contain a good measure of **Stoic** resonance. He held that the entirety of what there is is one substance, with both physical and mental aspects, and that all events are deterministically governed in a way that is accessible to rationality. Thus, like the Stoics, Spinoza held that there is a pervasive rationality ordering all that is, and that knowledge of that rational order enables us to escape from the agitation and discomfort of frustration, anger, envy and other painful affects. This is not simply resignation. It is the enjoyment of the freedom that comes with having a correct understanding of what must be. This is an understanding through which we come closest to understanding God as the cause of all that is in the intelligible, necessary order of the world. In living our lives through this understanding, we are most self-determining because it is reason that ultimately accounts for the order of things, and it is through reason that we are capable of being self-governing rather than moved by what is external to us. We most fully actualise our nature in leading a life of rational activity. And, what most fully actualises our nature is the cause of **happiness**. This is, in some respects, reminiscent of

Aristotle's notion of the 'naturally pleasing' in Books I and X of *Nicomachean Ethics* as well as of numerous Stoic thinkers' views. The more active we are (in contrast to being passive) the more self-determining we are. But this self-determination is not simply a matter of doing what one wants. Instead, it involves being moved by our own understanding rather than being motivated by passions and desires external to us as intelligent individuals. We thereby act on the basis of our nature instead of on the basis of what happens to us. To the extent that we have an adequate understanding of reality, we also have an understanding of what is good and what is evil. That is not a matter of preference or affect or convention. It is a matter of insight into our nature and the larger order of things of which our own individuality is just one finite mode.

Spinoza's treatment of ethics is not directly concerned with the permissibility or rightness or wrongness of specific types of actions. It is an articulation of a conception of human nature as part of the metaphysics of reality as a whole. We act best and live best when we act and live through a comprehension of the necessity of things. Any other approach to life is alienated from reality and enslaved to passions and desires that are not expressions of our rationality. As indicated, the view that self-determination is rational self-mastery and that it is pleasing to us has roots in ancient Stoicism, and it supported numerous branches of **rationalist** ethics, including **Kant's**.

See **virtue-centred** ethics

Further reading: Spinoza 1994

state of nature: In a number of important ethical and political theories the state of nature represents the pre-civil condition of human beings, a condition in which they have natural **rights** and liberties but where there is no political authority and there are no political institutions. In the state of nature the law of nature (variously construed by different thinkers) is the only law. Theorists have used the notion of a state of nature as a basis for accounts of what political authority and institutions are legitimate. They argue that human nature and the conditions of mankind in the state of nature supply the grounds for explicating the basis of the legitimacy of political authority and the grounds of obedience.

The state of nature is usually understood as a precarious condition from which rational agents will emerge on the basis of a social contract indicative of their endorsement of a specific form of political sovereignty and fundamental moral principles as well. However, in the work of some theorists (**Rousseau,** for example), the state of nature is used as part of a strategy of bringing into relief the corruptions of social and political life by showing what human beings are like when they are not living in an environment that motivates envy and competition for honours and power. There is a simplicity and **happiness** in the state of nature that is not found in the civil condition, which so easily brings with it the corruptions of wealth, dependence on others, and different statuses. At the same time, Rousseau held that in a civil social world human beings are able to develop their abilities and engage in excellent activities and modes of self-determination that are possible only in civil life. His account allows more scope for valuing the state of nature and for feeling apprehension about the civil state than do the views of say, **Hobbes** and **Locke**. In any case, whether or not a theorist purports to be describing an actual historical condition, the notion of a state of nature or an 'original position' is a methodological instrument for identifying and elaborating basic principles of political justice and morally endorsable social arrangements.

See **contract theory, natural law, Rawls**

Further reading: Hobbes 1991; Locke 1988; Rawls 1971; Rousseau 1978

Stevenson, Charles (1908–79) American: His work presents a fuller elaboration of the emotive meaning of ethical language. This includes the practical influence of ethical discourse and the ways it encourages or discourages certain attitudes, choices and evaluations; and the ways it can influence the motives of those who are addressed. According to the **emotivists** one of the failures of **realism** is that it cannot account for the practical, action-influencing significance of ethical language. In order to explicate that, Stevenson emphasises the distinction between beliefs and attitudes, and the ways in which ethical language can affect the latter. The use of ethical language does more than just express the speaker's attitude or affect.

See **anti-realism, Ayer, non-cognitivism**

Further reading: Stevenson 1963

Stoicism: A philosophy with origins among the ancient Greeks that later had numerous important Roman exponents. Stoic thought ranged across a wide gamut, including logic, metaphysics and epistemology, as well as ethics. For the Stoics, **virtue** was mainly a matter of valuing things correctly – having the right attitude toward them. The core element of Stoic ethics is that virtue has a distinct and incomparable value, and that virtue is sufficient for an excellent and happy life. The Stoics recognised that various kinds of pain, suffering, failure and deprivation can powerfully influence one's **happiness**, but they also held that they *should not*. These are all things to be avoided or minimised, but virtue alone is what makes for an excellent and happy life. Even all those things in life that are preferable and enjoyable – such things as wealth, health and success at one's undertakings – do not have the kind of value that makes for an excellent and happy life. There are many things – such as wealth, health, fame – that are to be regarded as preferred even though they are not good in themselves, something unique to virtue. There is some **Socratic** resonance in the Stoic claims that knowledge is sufficient for virtue, and that it is through virtue that one's nature is harmonised. With the Stoics this meant being harmonised with reality over-all, not just achieving harmony in one's psyche. Virtue is largely a matter of rational self-command or self-mastery and not letting one's valuation of things be distracted by passions and appetites. Stoics did not uniformly condemn the passions. However, they *did* uniformly argue that the passions which are proper and fitting are the ones that promote the end of harmony between human beings as part of the order of reality overall.

It is to the Stoics that we largely owe the notion of all people being participants in a common moral order on the basis of all persons being rational. They expounded a moral cosmopolitanism that was important to the development of theories of **natural law**. Human beings are not only social beings, but they are also citizens of the world, not just citizens of this or that community or state. Later on, elements of Stoicism are reflected in several different types of ethical theorising including that of **Spinoza**, **Smith** and **Kant**.

See *ataraxia*, **Aurelius**, **Epictetus**, virtue-centred theorising

Further reading: Aurelius 1989; Epictetus 1948; Kant 1976; Smith 1984; Spinoza 1994

subjectivism: There are many versions of subjectivism with regard to ethics. What they share is a denial that there are
objective moral values or objective moral considerations.
This means that values are understood to be grounded
in feeling, desire, sensibility, choice, that is, in something
other than cognition or *a priori* principles. Subjectivists
are often interested in giving an account of the nature
and status of moral values rather than aiming to undermine the genuineness or authority of them. Defenders of
objectivism often argue that subjectivism does indeed undermine morality, that it does not leave morality undisturbed. That debate about the relation between first-order
morality and second-order conceptions of its status is an
important issue in **metaethics.** Subjectivists sometimes argue that moral considerations *matter* to us as they always have, it's just that subjectivism is the best account
of the metaphysical status of moral value and it is an
anti-realist one. Change and even improvement in moral
positions are not examples of an objective moral reality
being brought into view, but subjectivists argue that that
need not imply that commitment to our current values
amounts to no more than arbitrary preference.

In many cases, subjectivists rely heavily on the argument that cognition of moral reality, or moral facts
cannot explain the essentially *practical* dimension of
moral commitments, the fact that they motivate us to
act. They may argue that: (1) there are no moral facts;
and (2) even if there were, they would be of no significance with regard to action because a belief on its own
is motivationally inert, while moral commitments have
motivational efficacy. In turn, defenders of objectivism
will argue that subjectivism is no better off than **scepticism,** and its attempt to underwrite morality on subjectivist grounds cannot succeed. It undermines morality in ways some subjectivists refuse to acknowledge but

cannot evade. Thus, there is the debate over whether values are subjective or objective, and also the debate over the difference to morality that is made by the two views.

See **projectivism**

Further reading: Blackburn 1993 and 1998; Harman 1977; Hume 1975 and 1978; Mackie 1990; McDowell 1988; Smith 1984

supererogation: An act is supererogatory if it exceeeds what is morally required, 'above and beyond the call of duty' as it is colloquially put. In some moral theories, for example virtue-centred theories, there may be a conception of an ideal of perfect **virtue**, but it is not reasonable to expect people to attain that ideal. This does not mean that it is morally permissible to have only modest moral aspirations or to make only modest efforts. Rather, it is a way of acknowledging that moral **perfection** is perhaps not the appropriate expectation, though it is an appropriate ideal. This is not quite the same thing as supererogation, which is more a matter of exceeding what is required by moral obligation. Obligation may require each person to act in ways that promote the well-being of others, but to do so at tremendous risk to one's self might be supererogatory.

This sort of notion of the 'praiseworthy but not required' is not an element of every moral theory. A theory that did not include it would not be deficient just on that account. However, in moral theorising in general, it can be important to ascertain what should be expected of people. In doing so we might bring into view what counts as possible, permissible, but not obligatory (heroic) behaviour, and the grounds for regarding it as such rather than as possibly irrational or ill-advised.

Further reading: Kant 1976; Mill 1979

supervenience: Many theorists claim that the relation between moral and non-moral entities and properties is best understood as a relation of supervenience. In such a relation the presence of the supervening property (e.g. good) depends upon the presence of other, non-moral properties (e.g. relieving pain, promoting health, allocation of resources in accord with need, and so on). However, the relation between supervening properties and base properties cannot be expressed analytically and the supervening properties are not reducible to the base properties. Still, if anything else has the relevant base properties, the presence of the supervening property is assured. And, if there is a change in the supervening properties it is because the base properties have changed.

The relation of supervenience figures prominently in many areas of philosophy, such as philosophy of mind, aesthetics, philosophy of science, among others. For example, many theorists hold that conscious, experienced states of mind supervene on physio-chemical states and properties. The former are not altogether independent of the latter, but they can neither be defined in terms of them nor reductively explicated as 'nothing but' physio-chemical states and properties. How exactly supervenience is to be explicated is important because there seem to be several contexts in which there are relations of dependence between different kinds of properties where the dependence seems to involve some sort of necessity, but not logical or definitional necessity. **Moore**, for example, held that good is an objective, **non-natural** reality, but it does not just occur randomly. Things are good because of other, non-moral properties that they have, even though good is not exhaustively constituted by those other properties. It has its own distinct nature. The claim that values supervene has been made by **realists**, **anti-realists**, ethical **naturalists**, and **non-naturalists**. It is not a claim that is confined to just one type of interpretation of moral value.

The term 'supervenience' was introduced by R. M. Hare, in the development of his **prescriptivist** theory. He wanted to show that the prescriptive, evaluative significance of moral terms could not be accounted for by naturalistic interpretations of them. Anti-realists sometimes appeal to supervenience as a way of showing that prescriptivity is **projected** onto non-moral properties, but in regular and orderly ways. Realists will often appeal to supervenience as a way of giving an account of the objectivity of moral properties and their dependence upon other kinds of properties.

Further reading: Blackburn 1993; Brink 1989; Hare 1973; Sturgeon 1988

sympathy: In many moral theories sympathy is crucial to both the account of moral value and the account of moral motivation. 'Sympathy' is sometimes understood in a quite broad sense, as the capacity to enter into the concerns, responses, wants, interests and feelings of others, rather than being narrowly a matter of feeling for the distress of others. For example, the ability to 'put one's self in the other's position' is an example of sympathy. Fellow-feeling in general, and of several distinct types, can properly come under that heading. Both **Hume** and **Smith** regarded sympathy as crucial to morality, in large part, because it is through sympathetic response and imagination that we have concern for others as participants in a common moral world. They offered different interpretations of sympathy and its role, but shared a sense of its centrality.

In many **expressivist** theories of moral value it is argued that our judgements of what is good and bad, virtuous and vicious, and so forth are grounded in our reactions, our passions, more fundamentally than in cognition. Reason certainly has a role in deliberating about what to do and in the project of acquiring factual beliefs relevant to a moral issue, but our concern with moral issues is grounded in affect. Sensibility is the basis of the interests and the stances of approval and disapproval out of which our moral judgements are shaped. Moreover, sympathy can also be crucial to accounts of what could motivate people to act morally. It is not just essential to understanding values but also to explain the practical, action-motivating character of moral considerations. This is particularly prominent in **Mill's utilitarianism**. He argues that fellow-feeling and taking pleasure in the well-being of others, and being distressed by their suffering, are basic to moral concern. We could not acquire utilitarian **virtues** without sympathy. In many theories, both **cognitivist** and **non-cognitivist**, sympathy is an important issue simply because it is regarded as basic to how we regard others and their situations, even if it is not held to be the ground of moral value or moral concern.

See **emotivism, impartial spectator, moral sense, prescriptivism**

Further reading: Hume 1975 and 1978; Mill 1979; Smith 1984

teleology: In the way in which the term 'teleology' is used in ethics, there are two different senses in which a theory might be said to be teleological. In one, the notion of an intrinsic end and a notion of proper operation for human nature are central. **Virtue-centred theories** are often teleological in this sense. **Aristotle's** theorising is perhaps the best example. Teleology in this sense concerns the normative dimension of the capacities constitutive of human nature, and how their realisation is the cause of *eudaimonia* or flourishing. In the other sense, a theory is said to be teleological in contrast to being **deontological**. That is, it locates moral value in states of affairs, the consequences of action, rather than locating it in the agent's motive, character, or the intrinsic nature of action-types (e.g. lack of gratitude for a significant, well-intentioned benefit is wrong, simply because gratitude is owed in such a case). In this second sense, consequentialist theories are teleological though they are often explicitly not teleological in the first sense. Virtue-centred theories are typically not teleological in the second sense, and are often motivated by what are taken to be deficiencies of **consequentialism**.

See **perfectionism, practical wisdom**

Further reading: Aquinas 1966; Aristotle 1985; Foot 2001; Hursthouse 1999; Wallace 1978; Williams 1985

universalisation: Many moral theories hold that one of the key features of moral judgements is that they are (or are intended to be) universal in their applicability. That is one way moral judgements differ from matters of taste, for instance. There is no necessary connection between universality and **objectivity**, though objectivists will often argue that the objectivity of moral considerations underwrites their universality. If there are objective reasons why killing for fun is wrong, they are reasons that apply everywhere, not just in one or another context. **Kant** insisted on the universality of the **categorical imperative**, grounded in *a priori* practical rationality. Others have argued that a common human nature is the basis for the objectivity and universality of moral values and principles. Some Aristotelians and natural law theorists argue in this way. **Anti-realists** and **subjectivists** have sometimes insisted that their approaches, too, involve the condition of universality. **Hume** can be interpreted as appealing to completely general features of human sensibility as the basis for morals. **Hare's prescriptivism** takes moral claims to involve universality through the *meaning* of moral imperatives (in contrast to other kinds). 'You ought not deceive others' is universal in a way that 'You ought not serve whisky with quiche' is not. Moral claims prescribe in a way that other imperatives do not, and this is revealed by an examination of moral discourse. **Relativists** deny that there are universal moral principles or values, though it could happen just as a matter of fact that everyone agreed on moral matters. The relativist's position is that there are no objectively universal values or principles grounding that agreement. It is also possible to make a case for objectivity without insisting on moral rules or judgements being **absolute**. Whether a judgement applies universally may depend upon what the facts are. The considerations supporting a judgement in one setting may not be present in another even quite like it in many respects. This is especially evident in **utilitarian** thinking.

Further reading: Donagan 1977; Hume 1975 and 1978; Kant 1976; Nagel 1970

utilitarianism: In some moral theories 'utility' is the name of what is to be aimed at in moral decision and action. Different theories interpret utility differently. It should be noted that while the vast majority of the treatment of utilitarianism concerns the hedonistic **naturalism** of thinkers such as **Bentham** and **Mill**, there are utilitarian theories that do not involve a **hedonist** conception of good, and that are not even naturalistic theories. **G. E. Moore**'s moral theory is a version of ideal utilitarianism. Its conception of good is **non-natural** and non-hedonist, but it is crucial to his moral theory that we are to act with a view to maximising the good. Utilitarian theories are **consequentialist** in form. Right action (**act-utilitarianism**) or a right rule (**rule-utilitarianism**) is that which has the best (most utilitarianly desirable) consequences. Utilitarian theories face difficulties with regard to the issues of how to rank states of affairs in regard to utility and how to compare them. In light of this, some naturalistic utilitarians argue that we should ascertain utility by examining people's revealed preferences (on the basis of how they act) rather than trying to compare the utility experienced by different individuals (e.g. the pleasure they find in different states of affairs). In spite of those difficulties utilitarians often argue that any plausible moral theory must assign a central place to the values of states of affairs and the differences made by actions. A theory that does not do so will fail to be responsive to overall considerations of human welfare, and on account of that, will be defective.

See **preference-utilitarianism, Sidgwick, Singer**

Further reading: Bentham 1996; Mill 1979; Moore 1994; Sidgwick 1981; Singer 1993; Smart and Williams 1973

Veatch, Henry B. (1911–99) American: Veatch defended a broadly Aristotelian conception of ethics including a perfectionist conception of human nature and a realist interpretation of moral claims. This was before the recent rekindling of interest in virtue-centred approaches. He was also a defender of natural law and he argued that the rationality of ethics depends upon its being grounded in knowledge of nature. He did not mean this in terms of a scientific conception of nature. Rather, he held that the most plausible conception of nature includes the notion of a kind-specific telos for human beings and, accordingly, objective goods for human beings. He distinguished his view from Aristotle's by arguing that the latter's ideal of human perfection is implausibly intellectualist. Veatch held that ethical (practical) activity rather than contemplation is the proper end for a human being, though this centrally involves reason. Intelligent living is the best activity though that is not say that intellectual activity is the best.

See **practical wisdom, prudence, teleology**

Further reading: Aquinas 1948; Aristotle 1985; Foot 2001; Veatch 1962 and 1971; Williams 1985

veil of ignorance: This is a methodological device formulated by **Rawls** to define the condition of rational agents in the **original position**. Not knowing facts about themselves as individuals, except that they are rational, self-interested agents with the general capabilities and concerns of such agents, parties to the social **contract** arrive at basic principles and social arrangements from behind the veil. This is intended to ensure **impartiality** by denying agents the sorts of person-specific information that would motivate partiality, and securing advantages that are unfair because unearned. The condition of seeking to protect one's own interests while behind the metaphorical veil (in the hypothetical original position) helps ensure that agents will arrive at agreements on basic principles and arrangements that all agents can endorse. We can articulate what is fair through application of this methodology. Rawls describes his account as being in the social contract tradition of theorising.

See **Hobbes, Locke, state of nature**
Further reading: Rawls 1971

vice: A treatment of vice is appropriate in just about any moral theory, but it is especially important in **virtue-centred theories**. In that approach a vice is a state of character that is both bad and sufficiently fixed in the agent so that the agent habitually acts wrongly. A decent and even a good person can perform a wrong action or occasionally be weak-willed without having a vice as a stable disposition. The agent with vices *is* in that bad (morally disordered) condition. It has become his second nature and he regards his values as correct and his actions as right, while being in error on both counts. That is how vice differs from **weakness of will,** wherein the agent has sound values but fails to enact them. Also, the weak agent experiences regret for acting wrongly, while the vicious agent may find his own (wrong) actions pleasing.

There is certainly a place for a discussion of vice in **Kantian** or **utilitarian** moral theories but in them the moral qualities of states of character, whether virtuous or vicious, will be explicated in terms of a value or principle or criterion that is independent of an agent's character. In virtue-centred theorising the agent's character – virtues and vices – have a more basic place in the overall view of morality. Moreover, in this approach to theorising, virtues and vices are acquired. They are not simply present in us by nature though we do have certain propensities and tendencies grounded in temperament. If a person is unlucky in her natural temperament that on its own does not make for vice. The presence of vice depends upon how the agent chooses, acts and is motivated. Temperament influences that, but does not determine it. Thus, vice is voluntary.

See **Aristotle, practical wisdom, prudence**

Further reading: Aquinas 1998; Aristotle 1985; Foot 1978 and 2001; Wallace 1978

virtue: A virtue is an excellent state of character or intellect. A virtue enables a person to engage in good or well-ordered activity, either intellectual or practical. For some ethical thinkers, for example **Plato** and **Aristotle**, virtues are of primary importance in understanding good activity and a well-led life. For others, such as **Kant** and **Mill**, virtue is part of ethical theory but there are more fundamental notions such as the good will and utility, for Kant and Mill, respectively. For Kant, virtue is explicated in terms of how it reflects good will – morally sound volition. For Mill, virtue is explicated as a habit of desire in accord with which an agent is disposed to act in ways that promote utility. For theorists such as Plato and Aristotle virtue is a central element of moral theory, and the virtuous agent is the measure of good action. In the other approaches mentioned there is a criterion or principle of right action specifiable independent of the notion of virtue. According to **virtue-centred** theorising we should emulate and learn from the judgement and actions of the virtuous person, where this is not a matter of imitation, but rather coming to have the states of character, the sensibility, and the judgement and deliberative dispositions of that person. The virtuous agent can explicate the reasons for his actions, though this is not mainly a matter of following certain rules or principles. Of course, there are moral rules such as 'act fairly with regard to others', 'making deceitful promises is a wrongful practice', and so forth. However, what makes the virtuous agent's action right is not rule-following as such, but the disposition to act fairly and honestly, for example, and on the basis of an articulate comprehension of what fairness and honesty require in the particularities of different cases. In that respect, there is a crucial role for **practical wisdom** in much of virtue-centred theorising.

See **Foot, prudence**

Further reading: Aquinas 1966; Aristotle 1985; Foot 1978; Hursthouse 1999; MacIntyre 1981; McDowell 1979; Slote 1992; Veatch 2003

virtue-centred theory: This is an approach to ethics in which the excellence of the virtuous agent, rather than a principle or criterion specifiable independently of an excellent agent's character, is the measure or standard of moral soundness. This does not mean that one should simply imitate the virtuous agent. Nor does it mean there are no measures by which to ascertain who *is* a virtuous agent. Rather, it is the view that in order to act well and to live well, an agent must have certain states of character and intellect. These enable her to comprehend correctly the ethical significance of situations and deliberate and choose rationally what to do. A virtuous agent has correct understanding, good judgement, deliberative excellence, and follows through on what is chosen. An account can be given of why that agent's reasons for acting are correct reasons, but that account itself is most fully appreciated by virtuous agents because they are already disposed to recognise and weigh ethical considerations correctly. An agent lacking the **virtues** may not only be unmotivated to act on those reasons but may not even recognise them as right reasons, on account of her wrong conceptions of what is good. An agent with the virtues does not need to resist inclinations to act in wrongful ways; in being virtuous, the agent has those states necessary for acting well willingly and for its own sake.

Defenders of virtue-centred theorising often argue that while there are important general moral rules and principles, actual judgement in particular cases depends upon the agent's ability to recognise and appreciate the idiosyncratic features of those cases. Thus, virtue-centred theorising is often **particularist** in its conception of moral judgement. Accordingly, ethics is not codifiable. For example, fairness requires that we treat each person in accord with their legitimate claims, but what fairness requires *here* and *now*, in *these* circumstances, is a matter of carefully calibrated judgement concerning the weight of the morally relevant features of the individual case at issue.

In some of the most influential virtue-centred theorising virtous activity is the central element of *eudaimonia*, an excellent life enjoyed as such by the agent whose life it is. In that respect, the virtues have an important connection with **happiness**, even though virtuous activity is not engaged in only *because* it is conducive to happiness. Rather, the person who acts with a view to the just and the fine is best able to lead a life enjoyed as worthwhile and desirable for its own sake. In most virtue-centred theories there is a role for two kinds of virtue: virtue of character and intellectual virtue. The latter is relevant to morality because it is usually held that moral virtue involves sound understanding of the ethical features of situations and not just a disposition to act in accord with what is right. One could have the latter just by good fortune or good habits, but lack the comprehension of what makes right actions right, and lack the deliberative abilities to handle hard cases and situations in which there are conflicts between values.

See **Aquinas, Aristotle, consequentialism, deontology, Foot, MacIntyre, non-consequentialism, Plato, practical wisdom, prudence**

Further reading: Aquinas 1966; Aristotle 1985; Foot 1978 and 2001; Hursthouse 1999; MacIntyre 1981; McDowell 1979; Slote 1992; Veatch 2003; Wallace 1978; Williams 1972 and 1985

voluntarism: This is the view that values have their origin in the will, or in desire or passion, in contrast to being **objectively** real or objects of cognition or constructed or ascertained by reason. Quite different theories belong under its heading. Those which ground moral values in divine **will** are voluntarist, as well as theories such as **emotivism** and **prescriptivism**. There are narrowly **expressivist** accounts of moral value, such as **A. J. Ayer**'s, and broader, more textured accounts such as **Hume**'s. Both types are voluntarist, as are contemporary **projectivist** accounts. Some who defend non-theological voluntarism argue that morality may retain all the force and form of reason-giving, argumentation, assessment of claims as correct or incorrect, though values themselves are not grounded in or objects of reason. Projectivists need not hold that we choose which sentiments will be the bases of our values. That is, there are versions of voluntarism in which choice or decision may not be prominent though they hold that moral judgement is not grounded in reason. Even voluntarists who hold that value has its source in divine will make the point that God's will rather than intellect is the origin of moral value. This view is sometimes defended as a way of showing that God's freedom and power are not constrained by what reason understands as necessary.

The debate over voluntarism is persistent in the history of philosophy. In antiquity it was paradigmatically represented by **Plato** in *Euthyphro*, and medieval scholastics such as **Aquinas, Scotus**, and **William of Ockham** participated in it, the first making the case against divine voluntarism, and the latter two making the case for it. In that context the issue was important as a way of conceptualising omnipotence, God's knowledge and **benevolence**, the claim of reason to being able to make moral truth known to us, and the ground of the obligatoriness of moral requirements. One might argue that moral requirements are made known by reason, but it is because they have their ground in the divine will that they are obligatory. In the more recent and contemporary setting the debate continues most prominently in the form of **realist/anti-realist** disagreements formulated independently of theological considerations.

See **divine command theory, Euthyphro problem**

Further reading: Aquinas 1998; Hare 1963; Murdoch 1985; Quinn 1978; Sartre 1947; Scotus 1987; William of Ockham 1997

weakness of will: There is very extensive discussion of this issue in action theory, as part of the attempt to explicate the puzzling phenomenon of agents voluntarily doing things they believe they should not do. There are a number of different forms this can take. In one of them the agent completes deliberation, but does not follow through and enact his decision, because of the interference of a passion or desire. In another kind of case the agent does not deliberate or does not complete the deliberation because of the interference of passion or desire. The issue is important in moral theory on account of its relations to such matters as **voluntariness**, responsibility, **regret, practical wisdom** and self-mastery. It is prominent in **Plato** and **Aristotle**'s ethical theorising because they took on the **Socratic** concern with whether **virtue** is knowledge, and whether any agent could knowingly, voluntarily, act wrongly. If I have a correct understanding of what I am morally required to do, that is, I do not have a **vicious** character, how can it be that I should fail to do what I understand to be right? Is the failure indicative of something less than complete understanding, or is it indicative of something obstructing the understanding or what issues from it as decision? (I might not have vices but I may have less than fully-fledged virtues.) Thus, the phenomenon of weakness of will is related to questions concerning moral motivation, especially questions concerning the extent to which reason or knowledge can be motivational independently of desire or affect. There are also questions about the degree to which an agent is responsible for a morally wrong action if it issued from weakness of will.

Further reading: Aristotle 1985; Kant 1964; Plato 1992

will: Conceptions of the will and arguments over whether or not we have free will are important in a great deal of moral philosophy. This is because of the relation of the issue to questions about moral responsibility, voluntariness, and the locus of moral value. For the same reasons this is also true of the issue of the nature and significance of **weakness of will**.

In some **non-consequentialist** theories – Kant's is a good example – the will is the locus of moral value and it is interpreted as a rational capacity. **Kant** regarded the will as a rational capacity, the capacity to act in accordance with the conception of law. Thus, the will is that through which we respond to the authority of a principle of right action. There is scholarly dispute over whether **Aristotle** had a conception of the will, but it is clear that he held that action is not fully **virtuous** actions unless: (1) the agent acts knowingly; (2) chooses the action for its own sake; and (3) does so from a firm and unchanging character. In those regards he certainly seems to include voluntariness and perhaps something like will or volition in his conception of virtuous action. And his lengthy treatment of incontinence and impetuosity is a key resource in the discussion of weakness of the will. His use of the term *akrasia* has been followed in much of the work on the topic of weakness of will in general.

Mill gave an account of will quite different from those just mentioned. He interpreted will as a disposition or habit of desire. It was important to him to address the issue of the will because critics of **utilitarianism** raised the objection that we do not always act with a view toward pleasure. It seems that we often act in ways we believe we ought to act, without a view to expected pleasure. That is, we often act from volition, not from desire. This seems to threaten Mill's **hedonist** theory of value and human action. He acknowledged this, and replied that the will is not a separate faculty from desire, but that in willing to do something we do it from desire having become habitual. It can only become habituated from acts of that kind being originally associated with pleasure. **Hume** developed a theory of action according to which the liberty necessary for moral responsibility and the causal necessity required for adequate explanation of human action are held to be compatible.

In the various **Stoic** and Stoic-influenced moral theories, rational self-determination is a key feature. Even though the Stoics and many of those influenced by them held that the world is a deterministic system, rationality makes self-governance possible, and the best kind of life is one in which one's own rational volition is what moves an agent to act. In that kind of life the agent is least perturbed by what he cannot control and is most in command of himself.

Further reading: Aristotle 1985; Aquinas 1948; Aurelius 1989; Epictetus 1948; Hume 1978; Kant 1964; 1976 and 1980; Mill 1979; Spinoza 1994

William of Ockham (c. 1285–1349) English: Ockham's importance ranges across metaphysics, logic and semantic theory, as well as ethics. His ethics is a radical **voluntarism** denying that there are any natures, standards or ideals in accordance with which God must create and order the world. Ultimately, it is God's **will**, his commanding us to do X that makes X both morally right and morally obligatory. Any other approach would involve restrictions on God's freedom of will that are untenable because God's power is absolute. This does not mean that, given the way things are, God could command us to do just anything. Rather, God could have made the world in any order whatsoever, but given the order he created, what we are morally required to do is in accord with right reason. In that respect, reason is a reliable guide. However, what it is a guide *to*, the order it enables us to negotiate, is not in itself determined by reason; it is ordered by divine will.

See **Aquinas, Euthyphro problem, Scotus**
Further reading: William of Ockham 1997

Williams, Bernard (1929–2003) English: His critiques of some of the main approaches in moral philosophy (**utilitarianism, Kantian deontology, virtue-centred ethics**) have helped motivate large-scale reconsideration of the plausibility and adequacy of those approaches. Much of his criticism is grounded in his view that *the moral*, as a distinct, overriding kind of value and kind of thought is actually a misrepresentation – and a very unhelpful one – that leads to errors in moral psychology, moral deliberation, and distorts conceptions of moral reasoning.

Williams raised fundamental questions about how morality fits into life overall, and about the weight or authority of moral considerations. For example, we should ask if there are ways in which other kinds of value and other kinds of concern are not simply overridden by morality. His pursuit of those questions led into issues concerning the role of character, one's self-conception, and one's guiding concerns in responding to the various kinds of value in a person's life. Williams criticised utilitarianism and Kantian moral philosophy jointly for their implausibly abstract conceptions of moral agents and for conceptions of moral demands upon them that seriously misrepresent what people are actually like. Both approaches fail to account properly for crucial features of character, including elements of affect and of one's own identity and integrity as an agent. A more realistic appreciation of such things brings into relief the ways in which moral concern and moral reasons can have motivational efficacy and it highlights the excesses of impartiality built into utilitarianism and Kantianism. Williams also criticised virtue-centred approaches that rely heavily on **Aristotelian** resources. In that case, he found much to admire in the moral psychology, but also much to question in respect of the teleological metaphysics of morals and the **eudaimonism** that are part of many versions of that approach.

Further reading: Williams 1981, 1985 and 1994

Bibliography

Abelard, Peter (1971), *Ethica* (English and Latin), ed. D. E. Luscombe, Oxford: Clarendon Press.

Adams, Robert (1979), 'Divine Command Metaethics Modified Again', *Journal of Religious Ethics* 7, pp. 66–9.

Anscombe, G. E. M. (1958), 'Modern Moral Philosophy', *Philosophy* 33, pp. 1–19.

Aquinas, Thomas (1948), *Summa Theologica*, excerpted in *Introduction to Saint Thomas Aquinas*, ed. Anton C. Pegis, New York: The Modern Library.

Aquinas, Thomas (1966), *Treatise on the Virtues*, trans. John A. Oesterle, Notre Dame: University of Notre Dame Press.

Aquinas, Thomas (1983), *Treatise on Happiness*, trans. John A. Oesterle, Notre Dame: University of Notre Dame Press.

Aquinas, Thomas (1998), *Thomas Aquinas: Selected Writings*, trans. and ed. Ralph McInerny, New York: Penguin Books.

Aristotle (1985), *Nicomachean Ethics*, trans. Terence Irwin, Indianapolis: Hackett Publishing Company, Inc.

Augustine, Saint (1964), *On Free Choice of the Will*, trans. Anna S. Benjamin, Indianapolis: Bobbs-Merrill.

Augustine, Saint (1998), *The City of God*, trans. R. W. Dyson, Cambridge: Cambridge University Press.

Aurelius, Marcus (1989), *The Meditations of Marcus Aurelius Antoninus*, trans. R. B. Rutherford, Oxford: Oxford University Press.

Ayer, A. J. (1952), *Language, Truth and Logic*, New York: Dover Publications, Inc.

Bentham, Jeremy (1996), *An Introduction to the Principles of Morals and Legislation*, ed. J. H. Burns and H. L. A. Hart, Oxford: Oxford University Press.

Blackburn, Simon (1993), *Essays in Quasi-Realism*, New York: Oxford University Press.

Blackburn, Simon (1998), *Ruling Passions*, Oxford: Oxford University Press.

Bradley, F. H. (1876), *Ethical Studies*, New York: Oxford University Press.

Brink, David (1989), *Moral Realism and the Foundations of Ethics*, New York: Cambridge University Press.

Broadie, Sarah (1991), *Ethics with Aristotle*, New York: Oxford University Press.

Butler, Joseph (1991), *Fifteen Sermons* and *Dissertation on the Nature of Virtue*, reprinted in *British Moralists*, vol. 1, ed. D. D. Raphael, Indianapolis: Hackett Publishing Company, Inc.

Clarke, Samuel (1991), *A Discourse of Natural Religion*, reprinted in *British Moralists*, vol. 1, ed. D. D. Raphael, Indianapolis: Hackett Publishing Company, Inc.

Cudworth, Ralph (1991), *A Treatise concerning Eternal and Immutable Morality*, reprinted in *British Moralists*, vol. 1, ed. D. D. Raphael, Indianapolis: Hackett Publishing Company, Inc.

Dancy, Jonathan (1993), *Moral Reasons*, Oxford: Blackwell.

Donagan, Alan (1977), *The Theory of Morality*, Chicago: University of Chicago Press.

Dworkin, Ronald (1977), *Taking Rights Seriously*, Cambridge: Harvard University Press.

Epictetus (1948), *The Enchiridion*, trans. Thomas W. Higginson, New York: Liberal Arts Press.

Epicurus (1994), *The Epicurus Reader*, trans. Brad Inwood and L. P. Gerson, Indianapolis: Hackett Publishing, Company, Inc.

Firth, Roderick (1952), 'Ethical Absolutism and the Ideal Observer', *Philosophy and Phenomenological Research* 12, pp. 317–45.

Foot, Philippa (1967) 'The Problem of Abortion and the Doctrine of Double Effect', *Oxford Review* 5, pp. 5–15.

Foot, Philippa (1978), *Virtues and Vices*, Berkeley: University of California Press.

Foot, Philippa (2001), *Natural Goodness*, Oxford: Clarendon Press.

Frankena, William (1939), 'The Naturalistic Fallacy', *Mind* 48, pp. 464–77.

Gauthier, David (1986), *Morals by Agreement*, Oxford: Oxford University Press.

Geach, Peter (1969), *God and the Soul*, New York: Schocken Books, pp. 117–29.

Gert, Bernard (1966), *The Moral Rules*, New York: Harper and Row.

Glover, Jonathan (1977), *Causing Death and Saving Lives*, Harmondsworth: Penguin.

Green, T. H. (1883), *Prolegomena to Ethics*, New York: Crowell.

Griffin, James (1986), *Well-Being*, Oxford: Clarendon Press.

Grisez, G. and Boyle, J. M. (1979), *Life and Death with Liberty and Justice*, Notre Dame: University of Notre Dame Press.

Grotius, Hugo (2004), *On the Law of War and Peace*, Whitefish: Kessinger Publishing.

Hampton J. and J. Murphy (1998), *Forgiveness and Mercy*, Cambridge: Cambridge University Press.

Hare, Richard (1963), *Freedom and Reason*, Oxford: Oxford University Press.

Hare, Richard (1973), *The Language of Morals*, New York: Oxford University Press.

Harman, Gilbert (1977), *The Nature of Morality*, New York: Oxford University Press.

Hart, H. L. A. (1995), *Punishment and Responsibility*, Oxford: Clarendon Press.

Hegel, G. W. F. (1981), *Philosophy of Right*, ed. T. M. Knox, New York: Oxford University Press.

Hill, Thomas E. (1991), *Autonomy and Self-Respect*, Cambridge: Cambridge University Press.

Hobbes, Thomas (1991), *Leviathan*, ed. Richard Tuck, Cambridge: Cambridge University Press.

Hooker, Brad and Margaret Little (eds.) (2000), *Moral Particularism*, Oxford: Clarendon Press.

Hume, David (1975), *An Enquiry Concerning the Principles of Morals*, ed. L. A. Selby-Bigge, Oxford: Clarendon Press.

Hume, David (1978), *A Treatise of Human Nature*, ed. L. A. Selby-Bigge, Oxford: Oxford University Press.

Hurka, Thomas (1993), *Perfectionism*, New York: Oxford University Press.

Hursthouse, Rosalind (1999), *On Virtue Ethics*, Oxford: Oxford University Press.

Hutcheson, Francis (2002), *An Essay on the Nature and Conduct of the Passions and Affections, with Illustrations on the Moral Sense*, ed. Aaron Garrett, Indianapolis: Liberty Fund.

Hutcheson, Francis (2004), An Inquiry into the Original of Our Ideas of Beauty and Virtue, ed. Wolfgang Leidhold, Indianapolis: Liberty Fund.

Huxley, T. H. (1989), *T. H. Huxley's Evolution and Ethics with Essays on its Victorian and Sociobiological Context*, ed. James Paradis and George C. Williams, Princeton: Princeton University Press.

Kant, Immanuel (1964), *The Doctrine of Virtue*, trans. Mary J. Gregor, Philadelphia: University of Pennsylvania Press.

Kant, Immanuel (1965), *The Metaphysical Elements of Justice*, trans. John Ladd, New York: Bobbs-Merrill.

Kant, Immanuel (1976), trans. Lewis White Beck, *Foundations of the Metaphysics of Morals*, Indianapolis: Bobbs-Merrill.

Kant, Immanuel (1980), *Critique of Practical Reason*, trans. Lewis White Beck, Indianapolis: Bobbs-Merrill.

Kierkegaard, Soren (1971), *Either/Or*, vol. 1, trans. D. F. Swenson and L. M. Swenson, Princeton: Princeton University Press.

Kierkegaard, Soren (1972), *Either/Or*, vol. 2, trans. W. Lowrie, Princeton: Princeton University Press.

Kierkegaard, Soren (1973), *The Concept of Dread*, trans. W. Lowrie, Princeton: Princeton University Press.

Kierkegaard, Soren (1974), *Concluding Scientific Postscript*, trans. D. F. Swenson, Princeton: Princeton University Press.

Korsgaard, Christine (1997), *The Sources of Normativity*, Cambridge: Cambridge University Press.

Locke, John (1988), *Two Treatises of Government*, ed. Peter Laslett, Cambridge: Cambridge University Press.

Lyons, David (1965), *Forms and Limits of Utilitarianism*, Oxford: Clarendon Press.

McDowell, John (1978), 'Are Moral Requirements Hypothetical Imperatives?', *Proceedings of the Aristotelian Society*, supplementary vol. 52, pp. 13–29.

McDowell, John (1979), 'Virtue and Reason', in *Monist* 62, pp. 331–50.

McDowell, John (1988), 'Values and Secondary Qualities', in Geoffrey Sayre-McCord (ed.), *Essays on Moral Realism*, Ithaca: Cornell University Press, pp. 166–80.

McDowell, John (1997), 'Projection and Truth in Ethics,' in Stephen Darwall, Allan Gibbard and Peter Railton (eds), *Moral Discourse and Practice*, New York: Oxford University Press, pp. 215–25.

MacIntyre, Alasdair (1981), *After Virtue*, Notre Dame: University of Notre Dame Press.

MacIntyre, Alasdair (1988), *Whose Justice? Which Rationality?*, Notre Dame: University of Notre Dame Press.

MacIntyre, Alasdair (2001), *Dependent Rational Animals*, Chicago: Open Court.

Mackie, John (1990), *Ethics: Inventing Right and Wrong*, Harmondsworth: Penguin Books.

McNaughton, David (1988), *Moral Vision*, Oxford: Blackwell.

Maimonides, Moses (1956), *The Guide for the Perplexed*, trans. M. Friedlander, New York: Dover.

Maimonides, Moses (1975), *Ethical Writings of Maimonides*, ed. Raymond L. Weiss and Charles Butterworth, New York: Dover Publications, Inc.

Mandeville, Bernard (1924), *The Fable of the Bees: or, Private Vices, Publick Benefits*, Oxford: Clarendon Press.

Mill, J. S. (1979), *Utilitarianism*, Indianapolis: Hackett Publishing Company.

Moore, G. E. (1994), *Principia Ethica*, Cambridge: Cambridge University Press.

Murdoch, Iris (1985), *The Sovereignty of Good*, London: Routledge and Kegan Paul.

Murphy, Jeffrie G. and Jean Hampton (1988), *Forgiveness and Mercy*, Cambridge: Cambridge University Press.

Nagel, Thomas (1970), *The Possibility of Altruism*, Princeton: Princeton University Press.

Nagel, Thomas (1985), *Mortal Questions*, New York: Cambridge University Press.

Nagel, Thomas (1986), *The View from Nowhere*, New York: Oxford University Press.

Nietzsche, Friedrich (1966), *Beyond Good and Evil*, trans. W. Kaufmann, New York: Random House.

Nietzsche, Friedrich (1998), *On the Genealogy of Morality*, trans. M. Clark and A. J. Swensen, Indianapolis: Hackett Publishing Company, Inc.

Norton, David (1976), *Personal Destinies*, Princeton: Princeton University Press.

Nozick, Robert (1974), *Anarchy, State and Utopia*, New York: Basic Books.

Plato (1981), *Crito*, trans. G. M. A. Grube, in *Five Dialogues*, Indianapolis: Hackett Publishing Company, Inc.

Plato (1981), *Euthyphro*, trans. G. M. A. Grube, in *Five Dialogues*, Indianapolis: Hackett Publishing Company, Inc..

Plato (1992), *Republic*, trans. G. M. A. Grube, Indianapolis: Hackett Publishing Company, Inc.

Plato (1994), *Gorgias*, trans. Robin Waterfield, Oxford: Oxford University Press.

Platts, Mark (1979), *Ways of Meaning*, London: Routledge and Kegan Paul.

Plotinus (1991), *Enneads*, trans. Stephen MacKenna, New York: Penguin.

Price, Richard (1991), *A Review of the Principal Questions in Morals*, reprinted in D. D. Raphael (ed.), *British Moralists*, vol. II, Indianapolis: Hackett Publishing Company, Inc.

Prichard, H. A. (1912), 'Does Moral Philosophy Rest on a Mistake?', *Mind* 21, pp. 21–37.

Pufendorf, Samuel von (1991), *On the Duty of Man and Citizen According to Natural Law*, ed. James Tully, trans. Michael Silverthorne, Cambridge: Cambridge University Press.

Quinn, Phillip (1978), *Divine Commands and Moral Requirements*, Oxford: Clarendon Press.

Rachels, James (1986), *The End of Life: Euthanasia and Morality*, Oxford: Oxford University Press.

Railton, Peter (1986), 'Moral Realism', *Philosophical Review* 95, pp. 163–207.

Rawls, John (1971), *A Theory of Justice*, Cambridge: Harvard University Press.

Rawls, John (1997), 'Kantian Constructivism in Moral Theory', in Stephen Darwall, Allan Gibbard and Peter Railton (eds), *Moral Discourse and Practice*, New York: Oxford University Press.

Raz, Joseph (1986), *The Morality of Freedom*, Oxford: Clarendon Press.

Reid, Thomas (1872), *Essays on the Active Powers of Man*, ed. William Hamilton (facs. of 7th edn), Charlottesville, Virginia: Lincoln-Rembrandt Publishing.

Ross, W. D. (1930), *The Right and the Good*, Oxford: Clarendon Press.

Rousseau J. J. (1978), *The Social Contract*, trans. Maurice Cranston, Harmondsworth: Penguin.

Ruse, Michael (1986), *Taking Darwin Seriously*, New York: Blackwell.

Sartre, Jean Paul (1947), *Existentialisme est un Humanisme* (English), New York: Philosophical Library.

Scanlon, Thomas (1997), 'Contractualism and Utilitarianism', in Stephen Darwall, Allan Gibbard and Peter Railton (eds), *Moral Discourse and Practice*, New York: Oxford University Press.

Scanlon, Thomas (2000), *What we Owe to Each Other*, Cambridge: Harvard University Press.

Scheffler, Samuel (1982), *The Rejection of Consequentialism*, Oxford: Oxford University Press.

Scotus, John Duns (1987), *Philosophical Writings: A Selection*, trans. Allan Wolter, Indianapolis: Hackett Publishing Company, Inc.

Sidgwick, Henry (1981), *The Methods of Ethics*, Indianapolis: Hackett Publishing Company.

Singer, Peter (1981), *The Expanding Circle: Ethics and Sociobiology*, New York: Farrar, Straus and Giroux.

Singer, Peter (1993), *Practical Ethics*, New York: Cambridge University Press.

Slote, Michael (1992), *From Morality to Virtue*, New York: Oxford University Press.

Smart, J. J. C. and Bernard Williams (1973), *Utilitarianism: For and Against*, Cambridge: Cambridge University Press.

Smith, Adam (1984), *The Theory of Moral Sentiments*, ed. D. D. Raphael and A. L. MacFie, Indianapolis: Liberty Fund.

Spinoza, Benedict de (1994), *A Spinoza Reader: The Ethics and Other Works*, ed. Edwin Curley, Princeton: Princeton University Press.

Statman, Daniel (1993), *Moral Luck*, ed. Daniel Statman, Albany: State University of New York Press.

Stevenson, Charles (1963), *Facts and Values*, New Haven: Yale University Press.

Sturgeon, Nicholas (1988), 'Moral Explanations', in Geoffrey Sayre-McCord (ed.), *Essays On Moral Realism*, Ithaca: Cornell University Press.

Veatch, Henry B. (1962), *Rational Man: A modern Interpretation of Aristotelian Ethics*, Bloomington: Indiana University Press.

Veatch, Henry B. (1971), *For an Ontology of Morals: A Critique of Contemporary Ethical Theory*, Evanston: Northwestern University Press.

Veatch, Henry B. (2003), *Rational Man*, Indianapolis: Liberty Fund.

Wallace, James (1978), *Virtues and Vices*, Ithaca: Cornell University Press.

Wiggins, David (1987), *Needs, Values, Truth*, Oxford: Blackwell.

William of Ockham (1997), *Ockham on the Virtues*, trans. Rega Wood, West Lafayette: Purdue University Press.

Williams, Bernard (1972), *Morality: An Introduction to Ethics*, New York: Harper and Row.

Williams, Bernard (1981), *Moral Luck*, New York: Cambridge University Press.

Williams, Bernard (1985), *Ethics and the Limits of Philosophy*, Cambridge: Harvard University Press.

Williams, Bernard (1994), *Shame and Necessity*, Berkeley: University of California Press.

Wilson, E. O. (1978), *On Human Nature*, Cambridge: Harvard University Press.

Wong, David (1984), *Moral Relativity*, Berkeley: University of California Press.